MORE

Practice Papers for SQA Exams

Higher

English

ISBN 978-1-84372-872-6

Published by
Leckie & Leckie Ltd
An imprint of HarperCollins*Publishers*
Westerhill Road, Bishopbriggs, Glasgow, G64 2QT
T: 0844 576 8126 F: 0844 576 8131
leckieandleckie@harpercollins.co.uk www.leckieandleckie.co.uk

A CIP Catalogue record for this book is available from the British Library.

Questions and answers do not emanate from SQA. All of our entirely new and original Practice Papers have been written by experienced authors working directly for the publisher.

Special thanks from the author:

There are so many people, without whose help this book could never be written: first of all, for the skill, encouragement, zeal, and team-spiritedness of Leckie and Leckie; the acuity of Alison Campbell and her knowledge of film and TV; Catherine Thompson, Chief Examiner at OCR in Cambridge for her perspicacity and comprehensive understanding of literature and examination techniques; Dave McCartney of Highland Council for his sheer expertise in all matters linguistic; Michael Laing for his insightful discussions about language; and, of course, Kevin Cockburn for his everlasting patience, devoted encouragement and precision of thought. I should also like to mention a long-term close colleague and friend, Irene Khalil, who very sadly and unexpectedly died this year – her contribution to my ideas about teaching and the welfare of pupils knew no bounds.

Text acknowledgements

The following companies and individuals have very kindly given permission to reproduce their copyright material free of charge:

The Herald and Times Group for the articles 'Education must be a primary objective' by Harry Reid (Close Reading exam F), 'We must change our lives, not just our driving habits' (Close Reading exam H) and 'War on the car' by Rob Edwards (Close Reading exam H).

The Independent for the article 'Is time travel possible' by Steve Connor (Close Reading exam G).

Ian Bell for the article 'A fine curriculum that keeps on failing' (Close Reading exam F).

Leckie and Leckie is grateful to the copyright holders, as credited below, for permission to use their material:

New International for the articles 'After 27 years of plodding service, it's time for The Bill's last case' by Tim Teeman' and 'ITV to axe police drama The Bill after 25 years' by Chris Smyth (Close Reading exam E).

The Discovery Channel for the article 'How to build a time machine' by Stephen Hawking (Close Reading exam G).

Every effort has been made to trace the copyright holders and to obtain permission for the use of copyright material. Leckie and Leckie will gladly receive information enabling them to rectify any error or omission in subsequent editions.

Introduction

Layout of the book

As the name suggests, this book is a volume of *More* Practice Exam Papers for Higher English. Its sister publication (ISBN: 978-1-84372-781-1 *Higher English Practice Papers for SQA Exams*) is also available and contains practice exams A–D, worked solutions and helpful explanations, hints and exam tips.

More Higher English Practice Papers provides you with an exact replica of the SQA's Higher English exam papers as well as the answers, plus commentary. The layout, paper colour and question wording and level are all similar to the actual exam that you will sit. But the book also, significantly and most importantly, provides you with more than just the right answer: it gives you a detailed commentary on how these answers are arrived at.

The answer section is at the back of the book. The answers include practical tips on how to tackle certain types of questions, as well as details of how marks are awarded and information about what examiners are looking for.

How to use this book

The Practice Papers can be used in two main ways:

1. You can complete an entire practice paper as preparation for the final exam *either* by sitting one under exam style conditions – timed and without using any references or notes – *or* by answering the practice paper questions as a revision exercise, using your texts and notes to produce model answers. Your teacher may mark these for you.

2. You can also use the Topic Index to find all the questions within the book that deal with a specific topic. If, for example, you are having difficulty in answering questions on word choice, then just look this up in the Topic Index and find all the questions throughout all four papers on word choice.

Higher English – the assessments involved

Higher English involves three kinds of assessment: three National Assessment Bank (NAB) assessments; a Folio of writing; and the external examination. We are concerned here with the external examination but, first of all, since it's a brand new assessment, let's have a look at what the Folio of writing involves.

Folio of writing

For the folio, you have to submit to the SQA, by the end of April, two pieces of writing (essays), each of which must be from a different writing genre. Each essay will be marked out of 25 marks, and the total out of 50 will then be halved to give a mark out of 25.

One of your essays must be of a broadly creative nature, and one must be of a broadly discursive nature.

Creative

- A personal reflective essay

- A piece of prose fiction (short story, episode from a novel)

- A poem or set of thematically linked poems

- A dramatic script (scene, monologue, sketch)

Discursive

- A persuasive essay

- An argumentative essay

- A report

Your teacher will give you all the necessary information about the arrangements for your folio of writing.

The examination itself

Paper I (1 hour and 45 minutes)	Close Reading – two linked passages with questions, totalling 50 marks
Paper II (1 hour and 30 minutes)	2 Critical Essays from more than one genre, each worth 25 marks = 50 marks

The assessment weighting

The exam paper is worth 100 marks and the folio is worth 25 marks, giving a total of 125 marks. The folio, then, has a weighting of 20% (25 ÷ 125 = 20/100 or 20%).

Revision advice

Of course, routine, teacher-assigned homework is an important aspect of your school or college work, but it is also important to build revision into your work timetable. It's sensible to design a revision and homework timetable for each week in advance – remember to cover all of your subjects and to leave time for breaks.

Make sure that you have at least one evening free a week to relax, socialise and re-charge your batteries. It also gives your brain a chance to process the information that you have been feeding it all week.

Arrange your study time into one hour or 45 minute sessions, with a break between sessions. Don't let your break expand into 20 or 25 minutes though!

Try to start studying as early as possible in the evening when your brain is still alert. Some people find it advantageous to study for an hour before their evening meal, others prefer to work late. Try to study a different subject in each session, except on the day before an exam.

Before you start revising, make sure you have in front of you any necessary class notes, paper, pens and textbooks. Learn to keep yourself and any notes you make well organised – buy a lever arch file or a ring binder, colour coded for each subject. Buy an A5 or A6 notebook to record any vocabulary items with which you are unfamiliar – it is essential to build up your vocabulary. Many candidates fail the Close Reading because their knowledge of the meanings of words is so poor.

Be honest with yourself – it is too easy to pretend to yourself you're working when you're not! And you know it!

Close Reading question templates

These practice papers will also be a useful revision tool as they will help you to get used to answering exam-style questions. You may find, as you work through the questions, that they refer to a question type that you haven't come across before. In particular, you should learn how to recognise and answer Close Reading question **types**, so that they form a kind of template in your head for the answers.

Examples of Close Reading question types

Question type	How to answer
Questions that ask you about the meaning of a word or phrase or section of the article **Code U**	Try to (a) underline the piece of text which contains the answer; then (b) make sure that you put the underlined section into your own words. *You MUST answer all code U questions using your own words as far as possible. Failure to do so – that is, if you use the words of the passage – will gain 0 marks.*
Questions about word choice **Code A**	You **must** look carefully at the task set – it's most probably about establishing/conveying the writer's attitude. Go to the appropriate words or phrases that convey that attitude and work out the connotations (remembering all five senses – touch, taste, smell, hearing, as well as vision); finally, relate the appropriate connotation to the task set. Do not give the meaning of the word.

Questions about the effectiveness of imagery **Code A/E**	You should first of all deconstruct or unpack the image – that is, explain the literal meaning of the image – then go on to explain how well it helps to convey the key ideas in this context.
	As well as metaphor and simile, *imagery* can also refer to devices such as personification, onomatopoeia, metonymy. Always check that you have related your answer to the task set – that's how to earn marks!
Questions about sentence structure **Code A**	There are **several types** of structure to consider when answering a question about sentence structure.
	(a) Look for lists – often the answer involves a list, but also know the effect of the various kinds of lists – **for details about lists, look at the information about them at the end of this table**.
	(b) Look for repetition of words or phrases – to highlight meaning and/or to create a steady, rhythmical build-up to a climax; can also create tone.
	(c) Look for a long sentence followed by a short one – the dramatic impact often falls on the short sentence.
	(d) Look for word order which is out of the normal – an adverb or prepositional phrase (e.g. 'After that') placed at the beginning of a sentence, for example, or at the beginning of a series of sentences; such phrases can guide the reader through stages in the argument or indicate a time sequence.
	(e) Look out for questions that either build up to a climax or may be rhetorical, implying or reinforcing the point (or tone) being established.
	(f) Sometimes the sentence structure is a series of imperatives (or commands) that reinforce the point being made; look out for the use of the exclamation mark to signal commands.
	(g) Look for a sudden change in **tense** – the sudden use of the present tense can intensify the immediacy of the situation – emphasising that it is taking place NOW or indicating the drama of the situation.
	(h) Look for the use of tricolon – **again see the additional information at the end of this table**.
Questions about punctuation **Code A**	Know the function of all punctuation marks: colon, semi-colon, paired dash or brackets (parenthesis), single dash, inverted commas, question marks and exclamation marks.
Questions about language **Code A**	The term *language* covers word choice, sentence structure, punctuation, tone and imagery – so just look again at these question types above!
Questions about the link sentence **Codes U/A**	You must learn the following steps.
	(a) Quote the word that links back – look for words such as 'all this' or 'these' or 'therein' or 'therefore', etc.
	(b) Demonstrate the link back to the *idea* contained in the previous paragraph.
	(c) Quote the words that link forward to the *idea* of the new paragraph.
	(d) Demonstrate the link forward to that idea.
Questions about structure of the passage **Code A**	This is often a link question: follow (a)–(d) above applying the steps to the entire paragraph.
	But it could also be an introductory paragraph, one which concludes the piece or one which sets up/builds up to the conclusion.

Questions about tone or mood **Code A**	The *tone* or *mood* is likely to be sarcastic or at least humorous – though it may be ironic, sardonic (mocking), bitter, angry, etc. Whatever, the mood will be obvious.
	Once you identify the tone, you should treat the question as a language question, since tone can very effectively be conveyed by, say, sentence structure – that is, repetition of phrases at the beginning of sentences.
Questions about conclusions **Code A/E**	Look for:
	(a) a word (or idea) that signals summing up – 'clearly', 'thus';
	(b) the use of the word 'And' at the beginning of a sentence or paragraph – the word signals/draws attention to the fact that here is the final point and, by isolating it in a sentence by itself, it highlights the summative effect of the sentence;
	(c) an identifiable rhythm created by alliteration, lists, climax – are there any phrases or words inserted to allow the main point to be kept dramatically to the end?
	(d) any phrase or idea that is dramatic and/or memorable;
	(e) an illustrative example of the ideas that have been discussed – an anecdote that has the effect of summing up or making an illustrative point about the passage as a whole;
	(f) reference in the conclusion to an image/idea/word already used at the beginning of the passage that has a rounding effect and is summative in nature.
Questions about both passages **Code E**	Here you are asked either about **ideas** alone or **style** alone or both **ideas and styles**.
	You should also bear in mind that *style* covers all that *language* covers (word choice, sentence structure, punctuation and imagery). But you should also consider *tone* and use of *examples* or *anecdote*.
	The important factor in answering this question is to be highly specific: there are usually 5 marks for this question and it involves comparison – therefore you have to make at least two points about both passages – and each point must be supported by specific references.
	If you are asked about *ideas* and *style*, you have to (a) demonstrate a clear understanding of both passages; (b) make sensible, specific and perceptive comments on style; and (c) make some comments which clearly demonstrate the effect of the style – sensational, humorous, human interest, use of anecdote or illustrative examples. You can, of course, demonstrate the contrast in tone, if relevant, between the passages.

Lists

Let's look more fully at sentence structure when it's in the form of lists.

There are four basic types of lists – note the essential comment on effect in each case.

(a) Polysyndetic lists, where there are conjunctions between each item.

The effect is usually to stress that each item carries equal importance. It can also give the impression that the items are significantly and causally linked.

(b) Asyndetic lists, where there are no conjunctions between each item.

The effect is usually (i) to suggest range and/or variety of whatever is being discussed, and/or (ii) to create climax.

(c) Lists in parallel structure, where the pattern of each item (be it a word, a phrase, or a clause) is repeated – e.g. a verb in the infinitive + prepositional phrase: *To be beaten upon by the winds, to be drenched by the perpetual rain, to be surrounded in enveloping fog.* The effect is often climactic (working up to a final dramatic point) or again it may be to stress the range and variety of whatever is being discussed. This device is also known as **anaphora**: the repetition of a sequence of words at the beginning of clauses or sentences to create emphasis.

(d) Tricolon, where there are three items listed in a sentence – e.g. the American Declaration of Independence states: 'We hold these truths to be self-evident, that all men are created equal, that they are endowed by their Creator with certain unalienable Rights, that among these are Life, Liberty and the pursuit of Happiness.' Note here there are two tricolons – the final item is also a tricolon within the overall tricolon. Anaphora and tricolon are very effective rhetorical devices much employed by politicians because the rhythm they create contributes to a climactic and often dramatic build-up. You should consider these devices for your own writing!

General advice about answering Close Reading questions

Remember, the Close Reading paper is not a test of your ability to write formal English. You do not, therefore, need to write in full sentences – you can set out your answers in bullet points if you like. In the final question (where you are asked to compare the passages), however, it is wise to write fairly formally since you are being asked to justify your views in what is, effectively, a mini essay.

And also remember, since the Close Reading paper asks you questions which demand fairly concise answers, yours must not be long-winded. If your answer is vague, the chances are it is wrong!

Lastly, be reassured. In most questions, there is more than one answer possible. Markers are provided with most of these correct answers, but they are also told to mark positively – if they think an answer makes sense and is correct, but is not mentioned in the marking instructions, then they should award the mark.

Advice about Paper 2 answers

Introduction to literary texts

How best can you prepare for the Critical Essay part of the exam? Apart from reading the texts and writing essays in class and at home, what else should be done?

As well as becoming familiar with the texts that you have chosen, there is a great deal of useful work you can do before May. It is most important to know what the themes are of the plays, novels and poems you are studying. Don't just accept other people's ideas of the themes, but work them out for yourself – as long as you can base your answer on evidence from the text.

After you are fairly certain about the themes, examine the structure of the text. Novels and plays have an overarching structure in time: they have a beginning, a middle and an end. Occasionally they are structured middle>beginning>end (known as flashback or analepsis). As well as this overarching structure in time, the structure of novels and plays also involves (1) an exposition (introduction), (2) a development of conflict, (3) a turning point, (4) a climax, (5) a resolution and (6) a dénouement.

In the exposition, the narrative structure/point of view of the novel is established – is it third person omniscient, third person with focus on one character, first person? Also in the exposition, the author establishes the setting, characterisation, tone and symbolism.

Ask yourself:

Setting – where and when is the novel set and what is the importance of the setting to characterisation and theme?

Characterisation – what are the ways in which the characters are presented and what is their contribution to the portrayal of theme?

Tone – how does the tone/style contribute to the overall theme?

Symbolism – how does the use of objects/characters/weather/setting help to represent aspects of theme or suggest foreshadowing?

Each of these aspects continues to be developed in the remaining structure of the book or play (as in (2)–(6) above). Again, ask yourself: how does the turning point contribute to the outcome of the text? What about the role of the climax? How is the conflict – and the characters and the theme – finally resolved and how is 'normality' returned (the dénouement)?

In poetry, you must think about the various aspects of the structure of a poem – versification, rhythm, rhyme. More about the structure of poetry is explained in the answer section for the Critical Essays.

There is sometimes a debate about the relationship between the 'form' and 'content' of a poem: some maintain that the content of a poem is more important than the form while others say that it is the other way round. The easiest way to look at this issue is to regard the content as the ideas expressed by the poem; the 'form' is then the ways in which that content is expressed or portrayed. In other words, the form of a poem is the linguistic and poetic techniques used by the poet to express or portray the content.

But, as with plays and prose, you must work out the ways in which the structure or the form or the techniques of the poem contribute to the overall theme of the text.

When writing your Critical Essay, you MUST:

(a) **number your answer** (in the margin) to correspond with the question number in the paper;

(b) **introduce the material effectively and concisely USING THE WORDING OF THE QUESTION** so that the marker/examiner knows instantly and unambiguously that you are relevant; you should also use the opening paragraph to set your agenda, to make clear the structure of your answer;

(c) **structure your material appropriately,** ensuring that your answer will cover all aspects of the question asked and follows your agenda already set; note carefully the task – it is often in a two part structure. For example, 'Discuss the ways in which the dramatist presents the main character's internal conflict *and go on to show how it is used to shape the ending.*' A thoughtful consideration of this second part can gain you the 'A' grade you so desire!

(d) **make sure that paragraphs are linked;** make sure that ideas are linked and balanced – use terms such as *moreover, furthermore, however, on the one hand ... on the other..., not only ... but also..., although x is the case, y also is the case, nevertheless, accordingly,* to establish both linkage and balance;

(e) **make sure above all else that you remain relevant;** the greatest crime in this paper is irrelevance, where a candidate resorts to telling the story or blasting like grapeshot from a gun everything known about the text in the hope that some of the points made will impress the marker; ensure that each point you make relates to the question (the task) and use words such as *since, thus, hence, clearly, similarly* at the beginning of the paragraph to help indicate that you are proving a case;

(f) **avoid the formula: quotation + comment***; above all, avoid the formula: *quotation, this shows that ...*; work all quotations, unless they are very long, into the very structure of your sentence;

(g) **make sure you conclude appropriately** – *Thus ...* or *Clearly, it can be seen that ...* both signal a conclusion; thereafter refer back to the question and make the conclusion short without introducing any new material;

(h) **produce a cohesive and a coherent piece of prose** – *cohesive* means that it hangs together and is well-linked, and *coherent* means that the answer stands alone and makes sense by itself because it has been appropriately introduced, linked and concluded;

(i) **avoid all informalities,** such as abbreviations and/or contractions: words such as *isn't, wasn't, doesn't, can't, shan't* are not acceptable;

(j) **read carefully what you have written and make corrections** – this is a very important part of the exercise to avoid poor linkage, informalities in style and any of the other *don'ts* listed above!

Spelling

Being able to spell high frequency words, especially in Paper 2, is very important. Make sure you can spell: tragedy, rhyme, rhythm, soliloquy, relevant, humorously, separate, embarrass, necessary, sarcasm, definitely and loneliness.

Using quotations

Here is a simple guideline for the use of quotations: if the quotation is short – that is, fewer than two lines – it should be incorporated into your sentence structure. For example, let's assume that you are writing about *The Great Gatsby* by Scott Fitzgerald and you are making a point about the writer's use of setting. You write:

'Nick Carraway, the narrator, states that Gatsby's house is a "factual imitation", which suggests that he thinks that it lacks authenticity unlike the houses in the more fashionable East Egg. His use of "some" in "some Hôtel de Ville in Normandy" further indicates that Gatsby's house lacks significance and style – it is new and imitative, two qualities despised by those with "old money" living in East Egg.'

Note how the quotations are embedded in the sentence structure. Not only is that a sensible way of using quotation, it makes your text easier for the marker to read!

In the exam

Watch your time and pace yourself carefully – in both papers. You have an extra 15 minutes in the Close Reading paper, which should help.

These practice papers will help you to become familiar with the exam's layout and instructions, and could help you with the all-important timing.

Read the question thoroughly and carefully before you begin to answer it – make sure you know exactly what the question is asking you to do. If the question is in sections, e.g. 2*(a)*, 2*(b)*, 2*(c)*, read all the sections before you start writing. That way you will avoid overlap in your answers. Remember, this is Higher English and, whatever else, it is a test of reading skills. Don't misread questions.

It is less a question of luck than hard work. That is some sort of consolation!

Topic Index

Question type	Paper E Passage 1	Paper E Passage 2	Paper F Passage 1	Paper F Passage 2	Paper G Passage 1	Paper G Passage 2	Paper H Passage 1	Paper H Passage 2	Knowledge for Prelim Have difficulty	Still needs work	OK	Knowledge for SQA Exam Have difficulty	Still needs work	OK
Meanings of ideas/ summarising ideas	1(a), 2(a), 2(b), 2(c), 3(a), 3(b), 4(a), 5(a), 5(b)	7(a), 9(a), 9(b)	2(a), 3	9(a), 9(b), 9(c), 10	1(a), 1(b), 2, 4, 5(b), 6(b), 7	10(a), 10(b), 11, 12(a), 12(b)	1(a), 4(b), 4(c), 5, 7	9						
Meanings of words/ phrases/ statements			1(a), 5(a), 7		1(c), 5(a), 8		2(a), 4(a)	11						
Word choice	6		2(b)		1(c)			10, 12						
Sentence structure			5(b), 2(b)				2(b), 6	8						
Imagery			5(c)				3(b)							
Language	1(b), 4(b)	7(b), 8	1(b), 2(b)		3(b)		1(b), 3(a)	12						
Linking function			6											
Structure of paragraph														
Tone					6(a)									
Use of anecdotes/ analogies				8, 11	3(a)									
Conclusions		10	4		9	13								

Questions about drama

Topic	Paper E	Paper F	Paper G	Paper H	Knowledge for Prelim			Knowledge for SQA Exam		
					Have difficulty	Still needs work	OK	Have difficulty	Still needs work	OK
Questions about opening scenes	Q2									
Questions about characters	Q4	Q1, Q4	Q2	Q1, Q3						
Questions about endings/climaxes	Q1	Q3								
Questions about themes			Q4	Q4						
Questions about central scenes	Q3									
Questions involving comedy		Q2								
Questions about setting			Q3							
Questions about symbolism	Q2									
Questions about stage techniques				Q2						
Questions about conflict			Q1	Q3, Q4						

Questions about prose fiction

Topic	Paper E	Paper F	Paper G	Paper H	Knowledge for Prelim			Knowledge for SQA Exam		
					Have difficulty	Still needs work	OK	Have difficulty	Still needs work	OK
Questions about characters	Q5, Q8, Q9	Q6, Q8	Q6, Q8							
Questions involving short stories	Q6, Q7	Q7	Q5, Q7	Q7						
Questions about themes	Q7	Q5, Q6	Q5, Q7	Q6, Q7						
Questions about narration				Q8						
Questions involving humour				Q6						
Questions about setting	Q6			Q5						

Questions about prose non-fiction

Topic	Paper E	Paper F	Paper G	Paper H	Knowledge for Prelim			Knowledge for SQA Exam		
					Have difficulty	Still needs work	OK	Have difficulty	Still needs work	OK
Questions about essays/journalism	Q10	Q10	Q9, Q11							
Questions about biographies/autobiographies/travel books	Q11, Q12	Q11	Q10	Q10, Q11						
Questions about structure/techniques	Q10	Q9	Q10							
Questions about issues/themes				Q9						

Questions about poetry

Topic	Paper E	Paper F	Paper G	Paper H	Knowledge for Prelim			Knowledge for SQA Exam		
					Have difficulty	Still needs work	OK	Have difficulty	Still needs work	OK
Questions about characters	Q15									
Questions involving feelings/emotions	Q14	Q12, Q15								
Questions about themes including war/society	Q13	Q14, Q13	Q12, Q13, Q14, Q15	Q13, Q14, Q15						
Questions involving two poems		Q15	Q14	Q15						
Questions involving humour	Q13									
Questions about structure	Q16	Q13								
Questions about techniques				Q12						

Questions about film and TV drama

Topic	Paper E	Paper F	Paper G	Paper H	Knowledge for Prelim			Knowledge for SQA Exam		
					Have difficulty	Still needs work	OK	Have difficulty	Still needs work	OK
Questions about opening scenes and central scenes		Q19		Q19						
Questions about setting				Q16						
Questions about adaptations				Q17						
Questions about themes	Q17, Q18, Q20	Q16, Q18	Q16, Q19	Q18						
Questions about narration		Q17	Q17							
Questions about conflict			Q18							
Questions about endings	Q19									

Practice Exam E

Practice Paper E: Higher English

Practice Papers
For SQA Exams

**ENGLISH
HIGHER**

**Exam E
Close Reading**

Answer all of the questions

You have 1 hour 45 minutes to complete this paper.

Read the following passages and then answer the questions. Remember to use your own words as much as possible.

The questions ask you to demonstrate that you:

understand the ideas and details in the passage – **what the writer has said**
(**U**: Understanding)

can identify the techniques the writer has used to express these ideas – **how it has been said**
(**A**: Analysis)

can comment on how effective the writer has been, using appropriate evidence from the passage –
how well it has been said
(**E**: Evaluation)

The code letters (U, A, E) are next to each question to make sure you know the question's purpose. The number of marks per question will give you a good indication of how long your answer should be.

Scotland's leading educational publishers

PASSAGE 1

THE BEAT GOES OFF AS ITV KILLS THE BILL

In an article in The Times, *Chris Smyth discusses ITV's decision to end the long-running ITV series,* The Bill.

1 In a world of DNA fingerprinting on *CSI* and *Silent Witness* along with foiled terror plots on *Spooks, The Bill* was TV's bobby on the beat – familiar, dependable and, perhaps, a little out of date.

Britain's longest running police drama will end this autumn, ITV has announced,
5 after more than a quarter of a century as a proving ground for up-and-coming talent from Keira Knightley to David Walliams. *The Bill*'s ratings have slipped after a series of revamps that failed to lure viewers back. Last year, the most recent relaunch provoked outrage from fans when it ditched the distinctive theme tune which had become embedded in the nation's subconscious.

10 ITV denied that the decision to close Sun Hill nick was a financial one, saying the show was being killed off for creative reasons that would free resources for other 'high-quality drama'.

Peter Fincham, ITV director of television, called the show 'one of the great institutions of television drama'. He said: '*The Bill* has been a fixture on our screens
15 for more than 25 years and has been the home of some of the UK's best serial drama storylines, and a great showcase for scriptwriting and fine acting talent. But times change, and so do the tastes of our audience.'

He insisted that it would be replaced by one-off films and short-run series to give 'a wide range of high-quality drama' on the channel.

20 Graham Cole, who played PC Tony Stamp for 25 years until his character was written out last year, praised the 'wonderful legacy' of the show. 'A lot of young actors cut their teeth on the show. I first worked with Alex Walkinshaw, who plays Smithy, on *The Bill* when he was 14,' he told a TV website. 'It's been a huge employer over the years and the acting industry is really going to suffer. It's a very,
25 very sad day. I'm devastated for the actors and the crew.'

About 90 production staff are likely to lose their jobs as a result of the decision as well as the 18 permanent acting cast. The programme first appeared in August 1983, as a one-off play in the *Storyboard* series, under the title *Woodentop*. It followed the first day at work of the young PC Jim Carver, who was teamed up with
30 the more experienced WPC June Ackland.

Both characters became mainstays of the series for more than 20 years, alongside DI Burnside and the mischievously named DC Tosh Lines. Jeff Stewart, who played PC Reg Hollis for 24 years, reportedly attempted suicide after he was sacked in 2008.

35 Written by Geoff McQueen, it became a weekly series from October 1984. The show's rounded characters and ability to find drama in run-of-the-mill police work won a loyal following. Where US cop shows thrived on guns and car chases, *The Bill*

focused on muggings and robberies, grappling with issues of racism and social
deprivation. It went twice-weekly in 1988, and from 1993 was screened three times
40 a week.

It became an international hit, was sold to 55 countries, including Russia and China,
and was one of the most popular shows in Australia. A stint on *The Bill* was a rite of
passage for young actors. Knightley appeared in 1995, when she was 10, after a
teenage Emma Bunton in 1993. The show also boosted the early careers of David
45 Tennant, James McAvoy and Catherine Tate. Paul O'Grady – better known as Lily
Savage – played a transvestite in the late 1980s. Ray Winstone and Kathy Burke
have appeared, and Leslie Grantham and Denise Van Outen also guested. The show
won many awards and last month it was nominated for a Royal Television Society
award for Best Soap/Continuing Drama.

50 But in recent years, critics have found *The Bill* wanting in comparison with complex
US police shows such as *The Wire*. Schedulers have struggled with the show,
reverting to hour-long episodes in 1998 and experimenting with two pacey live
action episodes and the deaths of central characters. Last year it was moved from
the twice-weekly 8pm slot to a weekly one after the watershed, but in recent
55 months audiences had slipped below four million.

Talkback Thames, the company that makes the series, said it was 'devastated'. It
did not yet know how the show would end. Lorraine Heggessey, head of Talkback,
said: 'It is a credit to everyone who has worked on *The Bill* that the series will be
signing out on a creative and editorial high.'

PASSAGE 2

Tim Teeman, from The Independent, *argues that after 27 years of plodding service,
it's time for* The Bill's *last case.*

1 The mourning won't be sustained for the demise of *The Bill*. Put bluntly, this was a
long-running TV show that was respected – like an endurance runner – rather than
loved. It just went on, held on, kept going, with few memorable characters and
even fewer memorable storylines.

5 Despite its grindingly procedural drama, it held its place in the schedules with a
grim fortitude. The only thing that it was really known for, the only thing that gave
this viewer the slightest twinge, was the theme music – and not the awful trip-hop,
messed-up bilge of the final incarnation of the theme, but the original theme music,
which immediately became a classic when the show premiered in the 1980s.

10 As the show quickened, as the plots became louder and more sensationalist, so the
credits and music became more demented. Last year's final desperate reinvention
began with a highly charged story about race and knife crime.

It was ambitious and thumpingly written and directed. But, as with many stories,
you just didn't care at the end. The best thing about *The Bill* was showing the
15 reality of urban policing, but that didn't make for an involving continuing drama
(despite some babes and hunks and the odd love affair, it was never a soap). For
all its bangs, crashes, *The Bill* was boring. Soaps such as *Coronation Street* and

EastEnders endure because the characters and storylines connect with our emotions. *The Bill*'s characters never imprinted themselves on the primetime
20 psyche: Reg Hollis was no Den Watts, June Ackland no Peggy Mitchell. *The Bill* wasn't domestic and kept a damaging distance from characters and viewers. Like some officers – possibly, you might say, the best – it has given 27 years' loyal, plodding service.

Now it's time for the carriage clock.

Questions on Passage 1

Marks Code

1. (*a*) From 'In a world of DNA fingerprinting' to 'bobby on the beat' (lines 1–2), what two points is the writer making about *The Bill?*   **2**   **U**

    (*b*) Show how the writer's use of language in lines 1–3 highlights these points.   **4**   **A**

2. Read lines 4–12.

    (*a*) What points does the writer make in favour of *The Bill?*   **2**   **U**

    (*b*) What has ITV done in order to try to improve the ratings?   **2**   **U**

    (*c*) What reasons does ITV give for ending the programme?   **2**   **U**

3. Read lines 13–19.

    (*a*) By reference to lines 13–19, show how the director of television for ITV justifies his decision to end the programme.   **4**   **U**

    (*b*) Explain what, in your opinion, is his real reason for ending the programme.   **2**   **U**

4. Read lines 35–40.

    (*a*) According to the writer, what gave the programme a 'loyal following' (line 37)?   **2**   **U**

    (*b*) Show how the writer's use of language highlights the success of the show.   **4**   **A**

5. Read lines 50–55.

    (*a*) Explain what, according to the writer, finally brought about the demise/downfall of the show.   **2**   **U**

    (*b*) Explain everything that the schedulers did to try to save the show.   **2**   **U**

6. Read lines 56–59.

    Show by reference to word choice how effective you find the tone of Lorraine Heggessey's remarks.   **3**   **A/E**

    (31)

Questions on Passage 2

Marks Code

7. Read lines 1–4.

   (*a*) What do you think Teeman means by 'this was a long-running TV show that was respected ... rather than loved'?

   2   U

   (*b*) What is the writer's attitude to *The Bill*? Go on to show how he makes that attitude clear.

   3   A

8. Show how the writer's use of language in lines 5–12 reinforces his views of the programme.

   4   A

9. Read lines 14–24.

   (*a*) What reason does he give for claiming that 'it was never a soap'?

   2   U

   (*b*) What reason does he give for why soap operas work?

   1   U

10. To what extent do you think the last paragraph is successful as a conclusion to the piece? Justify your answer.

    2   A/E

    (14)

Questions on both Passages

11. Both passages treat the axing of the ITV police series, *The Bill*, in different ways. Which passage, do you think, presents the clearest case for ending the series?

    Justify your choice by close reference to **the ideas of the two passages.**

    5   U/E

    (5)

    Total   (50)

Practice Paper E: Higher English

Practice Papers
For SQA Exams

ENGLISH
HIGHER

Exam E
Critical Essay

Answer two of the questions

You have 1 hour 30 minutes to complete this paper.

You should answer TWO questions, each chosen from a different section (A–D). You must not choose both questions from the same section.

You may answer each question using texts by Scottish authors.

Make sure that you state the number of the question you are answering in the left hand margin and please take a new page for each answer.

You should divide your time equally between each essay.

The examiners are looking for evidence of the following skills:

- your ability to provide an answer relevant to the question asked and an ability to set out and develop a relevant line of thought

- your knowledge and understanding of the themes and significant, relevant aspects of the chosen texts, as well as your ability to provide detailed, supporting evidence

- your ability to show, where relevant, the ways in which writers' choices of form/structure/ language can be used to shape meaning, as well as your ability to provide detailed, supporting evidence

- your ability to evaluate the effectiveness of the text, along with your ability to provide detailed, supporting evidence

- your ability to communicate clearly and accurately, using appropriate written expression.

25 marks are allocated to each question.

SECTION A – DRAMA

Answers in this section should show, where relevant, detailed understanding of the theme(s) of the chosen text and should be appropriately supported by knowledge of relevant dramatic techniques, such as structure, setting, characterisation, dialogue (including, where relevant, soliloquy and monologue), plot, central scenes, climax, dénouement, as well as all relevant aspects of stage instructions, particularly the use of lighting, sound, stage sets...

1. Choose a play which has a highly dramatic climax.

   Show how the dramatist builds up to the climax and go on to discuss how he or she uses the climax to resolve the issues of the play.

2. Choose a play which has a symbolic opening.

   Show how the dramatist creates and develops the symbolism and go on to show how the feature helps set up the issues explored by the play.

3. Choose a play which has a scene central to the development of the play as a whole.

   Explain in what way(s) the scene is central and go on to discuss its importance to the development of the play as a whole.

4. Choose a play in which there is a scene where the protagonist undergoes a change of heart or mind.

   Consider carefully the build-up to the scene and what happens in it and then show in what way(s) it caused the protagonist to change.

SECTION B – PROSE

Prose Fiction

Answers in this section should show, where relevant, detailed understanding of the theme(s) of the chosen text and should be appropriately supported by knowledge of relevant fiction techniques, such as narrative technique, structure, setting, characterisation, symbolism, dialogue, plot, central scenes, climax, atmosphere, imagery...

5. Choose a **novel** which involves a rival's success or a manifestation of the supernatural.

   Show how either of the above events enters the plot and go on to show how it changes or influences our sympathies for the main character.

6. Choose a **novel** or a **short story** in which the setting is used by the novelist to warn us of events to come.

   Show how the writer establishes the setting in such a way that we are warned of what is to come later in the novel.

7. Choose **two short stories** which in their own ways have added to your understanding of the nature of people or society.

   Explain in detail how they have helped you to achieve this understanding and go on to evaluate which has done it more successfully.

8. Choose a **novel** which only very slowly reveals certain aspects of the main character.

   Show how the writer achieves this effect and go on to say how such a slow revelation of character contributes to the overall success of the novel.

9. Choose a **novel** in which the main character displays unusual determination.

   Show how the novelist establishes and develops this characteristic and go on to show how the characteristic affects your understanding of the novel as a whole.

Prose Non-fiction

> *Answers in this section should show, where relevant, detailed understanding of the theme(s) of the chosen text and should be appropriately supported by knowledge of relevant non-fiction techniques, such as structure (including sentence structure), narrative technique (including narrative voice), ideas, style, selection of detail, setting, symbolism, use of anecdote and/or evidence, climax, atmosphere, imagery...*

10. Choose a **non-fiction text** which is striking in its presentation of social values.

    Explain the values and go on to show the ways in which it is striking in its presentation of these values.

11. Choose a **travel book** that does more than describe foreign places.

    Show how the writer's presentation of foreign places is more than mere description.

12. Choose a **biography** of a character who was not famous and/or whose life was not conducted in the limelight.

    Show how the writer establishes and illustrates the personality of the character and go on to say how it was that your interest was maintained.

SECTION C – POETRY

> *Answers in this section should show, where relevant, detailed understanding of the theme(s) of the chosen poem(s) and should be appropriately supported by knowledge of relevant poetic techniques, such as structure (including verse form, rhythm, rhyme), sound, mood, tone, contrast, setting, characterisation, symbolism, synecdoche, climax, atmosphere, imagery, word choice...*

13. Choose a poem which celebrates or satirises an aspect of society.

    Show how the poet's use of language enables him or her to achieve either of these two effects.

14. Choose a poem which reveals feelings very similar to your own.

   Discuss how the techniques employed by the poet reveal feelings that are 'interior' and even personal to the poet but that you can share.

15. Choose a poem that creates a character whom you can almost recognise.

   Show how the poet has used various poetic techniques to make the character feel real to you.

16. Choose a poem the structure of which is essential to the effects created.

   Explain the ways in which the structure has made the poem successful for you.

SECTION D – FILM AND TV DRAMA

Answers in this section should show, where relevant, detailed understanding of the theme(s) of the chosen texts, and should be appropriately supported by knowledge of relevant film and TV drama techniques, such as structure, setting, characterisation, dialogue, plot, symbolism, synecdoche, editing/montage, sound/soundtrack, mise en scène (such as lighting, colour, use of camera, costume, props), mood, casting, genre.

17. Choose **a film** or **TV drama*** which deals with a subject close to your own experience.

   Briefly describe the subject involved and go on to show how successfully the film or programme makers have presented the subject for you.

18. Choose **a film** or **TV drama*** which portrays dysfunctional family life.

   Show how the film or programme makers reveal the family concerned and discuss the extent to which the theme(s) has/have been successfully portrayed.

19. Choose **a film** or **TV drama*** the ending of which depends, for its credibility, on the use of symbolism.

   Discuss the film or programme makers' use of symbolism at the end and go on to show to what extent it successfully concluded the theme.

20. Choose **a film** or **TV drama*** which explores a serious issue by means of humour.

   Discuss how the film or programme makers exploited humour and go on to say how that contributed to the seriousness of the theme.

*'TV drama' includes a single play, a series or a serial.

Practice Exam F

Practice Paper F: Higher English

Practice Papers
For SQA Exams

ENGLISH
HIGHER

Exam F
Close Reading

Answer all of the questions

You have 1 hour 45 minutes to complete this paper.

Read the following passages and then answer the questions. Remember to use your own words as much as possible.

The questions ask you to show that you:

understand the ideas and details in the passage – **what the writer has said**
(**U**: Understanding)

can identify the techniques the writer has used to express these ideas – **how it has been said**
(**A**: Analysis)

can comment on how effective the writer has been, using appropriate evidence from the passage – **how well it has been said**
(**E**: Evaluation)

The code letters (U, A, E) are next to each question to make sure you know the question's purpose. The number of marks per question will give you a good indication of how long your answer should be.

Scotland's leading educational publishers

PASSAGE 1

A FINE CURRICULUM THAT KEEPS ON FAILING

In the following article from The Herald, *Ian Bell considers the nature of the Scottish education curriculum and its examination system.*

1   Education is a wonderful idea – we should try it one day. Learning by bitter
    experience is getting us nowhere, as best I can tell, especially where education
    policy is concerned. But what do I know? I have – somewhere, God knows how, or
    even why – an education.

5   Mine is an older model. Some would swear by it still. On behalf of the less lucky
    members of my generation, I might be inclined to swear at it. They were chewed up
    and spat out, poor souls, on a kind of Darwinian survival course shaped around the
    knack of feeling well enough, resistant to nerves, and with all the easy fluency of a
    truculent parrot, at the moment someone said: 'You may turn over your paper.'

10 Heinous as it sounds, and is, I liked exams. By that I mean, and freely confess, that
    vacuum-packing my head for a fortnight prior to a quiz on those subjects about
    which I had a clue – anything else exposed the plan's flaw – was my preference. It
    was better than working, better than a year-round tedium of what we used to call
    'stuff'. As in: what did you learn in school today? Stuff.

15 'Bloke called Ohm. He's got a Law, apparently. And the Germans make up these
    enormous words. And it turns out the First World War – who'd have guessed? – had
    "origins". And glaciation used to be a big deal. And we've got a book called Physics
    is Fun but can't find a single joke. Ask me later – try 40 years – about algebra.'

    You think I'm kidding? I was what elegant Americans call a scam artist, facile in the
20 proper sense. The epitaph for my entire educational career would read: 'He got
    away with it.' Real learning, for its own sake, was a leisure pursuit conducted well
    away from school and relevant only when it came to conning the exam-setter who
    persisted with the Shakespeare question some of us always knew was coming. The
    real test was how to handle the test.

25 I kept it up, in one form or another, until they were patting my head at the
    University of Edinburgh to certify that, truly, I had got away with it royally. But
    educated? Equipped? 'Rounded'? Qualified for anything other than passing exams?
    On those questions, the candidate fails.

    I can read, write, add and subtract almost as well as I could when I was 16. The
30 rest – O-grades, Highers, Edinburgh's piece of paper – is chaff. Now and then,
    usually during the arts questions on University Challenge, a piece of debris will
    surface as proof that I didn't spend 16 years in a coma. But it's a very small return
    on the investment made.

    The poor joke is that I was one of the lucky ones. Hundreds of good minds of my
35 acquaintance went to waste like crops flattened by the great educational harvester.
    It is in no sense false modesty, not from this quarter, to say that too many people
    smarter than me did not survive a good pedagogical* threshing. Lives were ruined,
    odds were slashed, chances denied. And why?

40 The answer is straightforward: screw this up and your parents will, no matter what they pretend, be disappointed. Screw this up and your life's course will, despite all the consoling lies, be altered. Screw this up and you can kiss all your hopes and dreams goodbye.

Some people, terribly well-educated people, even hold that we should have them screwing up when they are barely more than infants. First test, then test and test
45 again. It's for their own good, you see. We need to know 'how they are doing' so that, if needs be, 'they can be helped'. Right. My own tawdry claim is that I never believed a word of it. Fail means fail.

Few people have a bad word to say about Scotland's Curriculum for Excellence. The language is a touch aspirational, but that's a quibble. Equipping youngsters with the
50 autodidactic gift, showing them that fact-retention is not knowledge, enabling them to see that problem-solving is the foundation of education: these, rather than the hamster wheel of testing, are fundamental. Yet can we get a reform that has succeeded in primary schools up and working among teenagers?

Apparently not. Teachers complain, apparently with justice, that nothing is ready
55 and that they too have some learning to do. They too must be equipped, or even informed – for such is one complaint – of the areas to be covered in the new curriculum. Why is there a lack of preparedness? May as well ask why there is a need for reform. Part of that has to do, to my untutored eye, with a failure to decide what we want from schools, and how it is to be achieved. But since no-one,
60 it seems, is arguing over the need to reform, the failure, then, to solve mere organisational issues is hugely depressing and damaging. Maybe this is the inevitable consequence of the education system that we all knew and failed to love.

*pedagogical means strategies/methodology involved in teaching.

PASSAGE 2

EDUCATION MUST BE PRIMARY OBJECTIVE

In the following article from The Herald, *Harry Reid considers the importance of education along with the possibility that it can be wasted on the young.*

1 Earlier this year I attended the 75th birthday party of the eminent historian Professor James Campbell. It wasn't really a party; it was a day of academic papers, presented by some of Campbell's distinguished former students for the education of a large audience of others, such as myself, who had also benefited
5 from the teaching of this very clever man.

Campbell taught me when I was 19 and 20 and, during the course of the day, I reflected on how much more I might have learned from this fine scholar if I had just been a bit older, a bit more mature.

Inevitable future cutbacks will mean quite a few teenagers will not be going to
10 university when they are qualified to do so. Yet it might be better for them, and indeed their country, if they postpone going to university until middle age and mid-career.

Shortly after the Campbell event, I found myself talking to a pleasant primary school teacher who had just retired. Latterly she had been teaching in Easterhouse,
15 and her conversation was something of a wake-up call for me, for I can have rather airy-fairy and high-falutin ideas about the nature and purpose of education.

I don't wish to present a false antithesis*, but, important as tertiary and secondary education are, the most important sector by far is primary education. This is where priority investment is essential; this is where we must help those who are already
20 disadvantaged, even before they have started properly on life's long journey.

Eminent scholars, dedicated teachers, excellent universities – all these can make a huge difference at various stages of life, but the biggest influence on educational attainment surely remains the domestic background of the pupil. If we are still a very unequal society, and unfortunately the evidence is that we are, then the single
25 largest cause must be the acute disparities in young children's home backgrounds. Many children go on to do well at school if they come from somewhere where education is valued, where the parent or parents are supportive, and where there is at least a modicum of space and quiet for study. For too many youngsters in our country, however, such simple requirements remain a utopian fantasy.

30 I am not proposing social engineering. I am just pointing out that at the primary stage of education, many children start 'failing' through no fault of their own. And primary education is now even more crucial than before because – although this can be exaggerated – television and computer games, and even cell phones and calculators, hardly aid the development of cognitive awareness and thinking skills.

35 Education can provide enormous benefits not just to the individual recipient of the education, but to our wider society. If many children are doomed, almost from the start, to miss out on these benefits, then that is the single most pressing problem we face.

And yet, in broad terms, our society regards education as only about a quarter as
40 important as health and social security. We spend roughly four times more on health care and social security than on education. This is a shameful and scandalous distortion of the true priorities of a civilised and improving society. In an ideal world, we would spend at least as much on education as on the social services. But how do we try to achieve an ideal world? Through education.

45 When I was a primary pupil in Aberdeen, I was taught that the 10 year-old Keir Hardie, after 12-hour shifts down the pit in Lanarkshire, struggled to teach himself to read and write and count with his slate and chalk when he was desperately tired after labouring in atrocious conditions.

Whether there was an element of salutary myth in this doesn't matter. We were
50 being told that education was the most precious thing of all, and that we were deeply privileged.

*A false antithesis is to suggest that there are only two opposing options, when in fact there could be more options or, indeed, the two ideas are not really opposites.

Questions on Passage 1

Marks Code

1. Read lines 1–4.

    (*a*) What do you think Bell means by 'Education is a wonderful thing – we should try it one day' (line 1)?

    2   U

    (*b*) Show how the writer's use of language helps convey the tone of the first paragraph.

    4   A

2. Read lines 5–9.

    (*a*) What, do you think, is Bell's attitude to his own education?

    1   U

    (*b*) Show how his use of word choice and sentence structure highlights that attitude.

    4   A

3. Read lines 10–14.

    What reasons does the writer give for liking exams?

    3   U

4. Read lines 19–24.

    How effective, in your opinion, is the final sentence as a conclusion to this paragraph?

    3   A/E

5. Read lines 25–38.

    (*a*) What does the writer mean by 'I had got away with it royally' (line 26)?

    2   U

    (*b*) Show how the writer's use of sentence structure in lines 26–27 draws attention to what he thinks education should involve.

    3   A

    (*c*) Show how his use of imagery in lines 29–38 makes clear his unfavourable view of his education at school and university. (You should restrict your answer to one image only.)

    2   A

6. 'The answer is straightforward' (line 39). Explain the ways in which this clause performs an important function in the writer's argument.

    3   U

7. Read lines 48–62.

    What exactly does Bell suggest is 'the inevitable consequence of the education system we all knew and failed to love' (lines 61–62)?

    3   U

    (30)

Questions on Passage 2

Marks Code

8. How effective do you consider the anecdote (lines 1–8) concerning Professor James Campbell's 75th birthday party? Justify your answer. **2 A/E**

9. Read lines 17–29.

    (*a*) What reasons does the writer give for regarding primary education as 'the most important sector'? **2 U**

    (*b*) What does he regard as the biggest influence on educational attainment? **2 U**

    (*c*) How does Reid go on to explain what he means by 'the acute disparities in young children's home backgrounds'? **4 U**

10. According to the writer in lines 39–44, how exactly do we achieve an 'ideal world'? **2 U**

11. To what extent is Reid's anecdote about Keir Hardie an effective way of ending this passage? **3 A/E**

(15)

Questions on both Passages

12. Both passages are about how the writers view education.

    Which passage, in your opinion, provides the most thought-provoking ideas about education?

    Justify your choice by close reference to the **ideas of both passages.** **5 U/E**

    (5)

    Total (50)

Practice Paper F: Higher English

Practice Papers
For SQA Exams

ENGLISH
HIGHER

Exam F
Critical Essay

Answer two of the questions

You have 1 hour 30 minutes to complete this paper.

You should answer TWO questions, each chosen from a different section (A–D). You must not choose both questions from the same section.

You may answer each question using texts by Scottish authors.

Make sure that you state the number of the question you are answering in the left hand margin and please take a new page for each answer.

You should divide your time equally between each essay.

The examiners are looking for evidence of the following skills:

- your ability to provide an answer relevant to the question asked and an ability to set out and develop a relevant line of thought

- your knowledge and understanding of the themes and significant, relevant aspects of the chosen texts, as well as your ability to provide detailed, supporting evidence

- your ability to show, where relevant, the ways in which writers' choices of form/structure/language can be used to shape meaning, as well as your ability to provide detailed, supporting evidence

- your ability to evaluate the effectiveness of the text, along with your ability to provide detailed, supporting evidence

- your ability to communicate clearly and accurately, using appropriate written expression.

25 marks are allocated to each question.

Scotland's leading educational publishers

SECTION A – DRAMA

Answers in this section should show, where relevant, detailed understanding of the theme(s) of the chosen text and should be appropriately supported by knowledge of relevant dramatic techniques, such as structure, setting, characterisation, dialogue (including, where relevant, soliloquy and monologue), plot, central scenes, climax, dénouement, as well as all relevant aspects of stage instructions, particularly the use of lighting, sound, stage sets...

1. Choose a play which presents a villain for whom we nevertheless feel sympathy.

   Show how the dramatist presents the villainous nature of the character and go on to show how the dramatist engages our sympathy.

2. Choose a play which is undoubtedly a tragedy, but which also contains comic elements.

   Explain the nature of the comic elements and go on to discuss the extent to which they enhance or detract from the seriousness of the theme(s).

3. Choose a play which you found to have a thoroughly satisfactory ending.

   Explain by reference to situation, character, and/or dialogue the means by which the dramatist creates this satisfactory effect.

4. Choose a play where the characters are presented with very real challenges.

   Show how the playwright makes real the challenges faced by the characters and the ways in which the characters deal with those challenges.

SECTION B – PROSE

Prose Fiction

Answers in this section should show, where relevant, detailed understanding of the theme(s) of the chosen text and should be appropriately supported by knowledge of relevant fiction techniques, such as narrative technique, structure, setting, characterisation, symbolism, dialogue, plot, central scenes, climax, atmosphere, imagery...

5. Choose a **novel** which deals with the theme of a love affair ended.

   Show how the novelist develops the theme and how, in the end, our sympathies for the characters are affected by the ways in which the situation is resolved.

6. Choose a **novel** in which a journey is central to the concerns of the text.

   Explain how the writer uses the journey to develop both character and theme.

7. **Short stories** often make a valid comment on aspects of human experience.

   Show how **two short stories** make such a comment and go on to show which of the short stories is the more successful at clarifying for you some aspect of people or society.

8. Choose a **novel** which reveals surprising aspects of the main character.

   Show how the writer achieves this revelation and go on to demonstrate how it changes your opinion of the main character.

Prose Non-fiction

Answers in this section should show, where relevant, detailed understanding of the theme(s) of the chosen text and should be appropriately supported by knowledge of relevant non-fiction techniques, such as structure (including sentence structure), narrative technique (including narrative voice), ideas, style, selection of detail, setting, symbolism, use of anecdote and/or evidence, climax, atmosphere, imagery...

9. Choose a work of **non-fiction,** the structure of which is important to your engagement with the text.

   Show how the writer's use of structure had the effect of engaging you with the text.

10. Choose a work of **non-fiction** which, though written in an earlier century, is still relevant today.

    Show how the writer's presentation of his/her material helps to make a valid commentary on some of today's social issues.

11. Choose a piece of **travel writing,** the language of which captivates and engages the reader's attention.

    Explain very briefly what you learned about the country and/or culture and go on to demonstrate the way in which the writer uses language to captivate interest.

SECTION C – POETRY

Answers in this section should show, where relevant, detailed understanding of the theme(s) of the chosen poem(s) and should be appropriately supported by knowledge of relevant poetic techniques, such as structure (including verse form, rhythm, rhyme), sound, mood, tone, contrast, setting, characterisation, symbolism, synecdoche, climax, atmosphere, imagery, word choice...

12. Choose a poem which, in your opinion, is a love poem.

    By close reference to the text, show how the poet uses poetic and linguistic techniques to engage the reader's interest.

13. Choose a poem which uses ambiguity to reveal its true meaning.

    Show how the poet employs ambiguous language with this effect.

14. Choose a poem which communicates the experiences of war.

    By close analysis of the language and poetic techniques, show how this has been achieved.

15. Poems are often written as a result of reflecting on intense emotional experiences.

    By comparing **two such poems,** examine the techniques used by the poets to convey the intensity of the emotional experiences.

SECTION D – FILM AND TV DRAMA

Answers in this section should show, where relevant, detailed understanding of the theme(s) of the chosen texts, and should be appropriately supported by knowledge of relevant film and TV drama techniques, such as structure, setting, characterisation, dialogue, plot, symbolism, synecdoche, editing/montage, sound/soundtrack, mise en scène (such as lighting, colour, use of camera, costume, props), mood, casting, genre.

16. Choose **a film** or **TV drama*** which deals with childhood experiences.

    Show how the film or programme makers make clear the importance of such experiences and go on to show the extent to which it manages to appeal to people of all ages.

17. Choose **a film** or **TV drama*** which depends on the use of flashback (analepsis).

    Show the ways in which the film or TV drama uses flashback and go on to discuss how the outcome of the story is shaped by its use.

18. Choose **a film** or **TV drama*** which explores the theme of missed opportunities.

Show how the film or TV programme makers use setting and characterisation to explore this theme.

19. Choose **a film** or **TV drama*** where one scene in particular is memorable.

Show how the film or TV programme makers build up to the scene and go on to show in detail how the techniques used in the scene gave you fresh insight into aspects of the text as a whole.

*'TV drama' includes a single play, a series, or a serial.

Practice Exam G

Practice Paper G: Higher English

Practice Papers
For SQA Exams

ENGLISH
HIGHER

Exam G
Close Reading

Answer all of the questions

You have 1 hour 45 minutes to complete this paper.

Read the following passages and then answer the questions. Remember to use your own words as much as possible.

The questions ask you to show that you:

understand the ideas and details in the passage – **what the writer has said**
(**U**: Understanding)

can identify the techniques the writer has used to express these ideas – **how it has been said**
(**A**: Analysis)

can comment on how effective the writer has been, using appropriate evidence from the passage –
how well it has been said
(**E**: Evaluation)

The code letters (U, A, E) are next to each question to make sure you know the question's purpose. The number of marks per question will give you a good indication of how long your answer should be.

PASSAGE 1

HOW TO BUILD A TIME MACHINE

In the following article from a Sunday paper Stephen Hawking asks whether time travel is ever likely to take place.

1   Hello. My name is Stephen Hawking. Physicist, cosmologist and something of a dreamer. Although I cannot move and I have to speak through a computer, in my mind I am free. Free to explore the universe and ask the big questions, such as: is time travel possible? Can we open a portal to the past or find a shortcut to the
5   future? Can we ultimately use the laws of nature to become masters of time itself?

To see how this might be possible, we need to look at time as physicists do – at the fourth dimension. It's not as hard as it sounds. Every attentive schoolchild knows that all physical objects, even me in my chair, exist in three dimensions. Everything has a width and a height and a length.

10 But there is another kind of length, a length in time. While a human may survive for 80 years, the stones at Stonehenge, for instance, have stood around for thousands of years. And the solar system will last for billions of years. Everything has a length in time as well as space. Travelling in time means travelling through this fourth dimension. But how do we find a path through the fourth dimension?

15 Let's indulge in a little science fiction for a moment. Time travel movies often feature a vast, energy-hungry machine. The machine creates a path through the fourth dimension, a tunnel through time. A time traveller, a brave, perhaps foolhardy individual, prepared for who knows what, steps into the time tunnel and emerges who knows when. The concept may be far-fetched, and the reality may be
20 very different from this, but the idea itself is not so crazy.

Physicists have been thinking about tunnels in time too, but we come at it from a different angle. We wonder if portals to the past or the future could ever be possible within the laws of nature. As it turns out, we think they are. What's more, we've even given them a name: wormholes. The truth is that wormholes are all
25 around us, only they're too small to see. Wormholes are very tiny. They occur in nooks and crannies in space and time. You might find it a tough concept, but stay with me.

A wormhole is a theoretical 'tunnel' or shortcut, predicted by Einstein's theory of relativity, that links two places in space-time; it is where negative energy pulls
30 space and time into the mouth of a tunnel, emerging in another universe. After all, nothing is flat or solid. If you look closely enough at anything you'll find holes and wrinkles in it. It's a basic physical principle, and it even applies to time. Something as smooth as a pool ball has tiny crevices, wrinkles and voids. Now it's easy to show that this is true in the first three dimensions. But trust me, it's also true of the
35 fourth dimension. There are tiny crevices, wrinkles and voids in time. Down at the smallest of scales, smaller even than molecules, smaller than atoms, we get to a place called the quantum foam. This is where wormholes exist. Tiny tunnels or shortcuts through space and time constantly form, disappear, and reform within this quantum world. And they actually link two separate places and two different
40 times.

Unfortunately, these real-life time tunnels are just a billion-trillion-trillionths of a centimetre across, much too small for a human to pass through, but some scientists think it may be possible to capture a wormhole and enlarge it many trillions of times to make it big enough for a human or even a spaceship to enter.

45   Given enough power and advanced technology, perhaps a giant wormhole could even be constructed in space. I'm not saying that this can be done, but if it could be, it would be a truly remarkable device. One end could be here near Earth, and the other far, far away, near some distant planet.

Theoretically, a time tunnel or wormhole could do even more than take us to other
50   planets. If both ends were in the same place, and separated by time instead of distance, a ship could fly in and come out still near Earth, but in the distant past. Maybe dinosaurs would witness the ship coming in for a landing.

But then we come up against the problem of paradoxes: paradoxes are fun to think about. The most famous one is usually called the Grandfather paradox, but my
55   new, simpler version is called the Mad Scientist paradox. This chap is determined to create a paradox, even if it costs him his life. Imagine, somehow, he's built a wormhole, a time tunnel that stretches just one minute into the past. Through the wormhole, the scientist can see himself as he was one minute ago. But what if our scientist uses the wormhole to shoot his earlier self? He's now dead. So who fired
60   the shot? It's a paradox. It just doesn't make sense. It's the sort of situation that gives cosmologists nightmares.

This kind of time machine would violate a fundamental rule that governs the entire universe – that causes happen before effects, and never the other way around. I believe things can't make themselves impossible. If they could then there'd be
65   nothing to stop the whole universe from descending into chaos. So I think something will always happen that prevents the paradox. Somehow there must be a reason why our scientist will never find himself in a situation where he could shoot himself. And in this case, I'm sorry to say, the wormhole itself is the problem.

In the end, I think a wormhole like this one can't exist. And the reason for that is
70   feedback. As soon as the wormhole expands, natural radiation will enter it, and end up in a loop. The feedback will become so strong it destroys the wormhole. So although tiny wormholes do exist, and it may be possible to inflate one some day, it won't last long enough to be of use as a time machine.

Any kind of time travel to the past through wormholes or any other method is
75   probably impossible, otherwise paradoxes would occur. So sadly, it looks like time travel to the past is never going to happen. A disappointment for dinosaur hunters and a relief for historians.

PASSAGE 2

THE BIG QUESTON

Steve Connor, Science Editor of The Independent *asks The Big Question: Is time travel possible, and is there any chance that it will ever take place?*

1   Two Russian mathematicians have suggested that the giant atom-smasher being built at the European centre for nuclear research, Cern, near Geneva, could create the conditions where it might be possible to travel backwards or forwards in time. In essence, Irina Aref'eva and Igor Volovich believe that the Large Hadron Collider
5   at Cern might create tiny 'wormholes' in space which could allow some form of limited time travel.

  It has to be said, however, that few scientists accept the idea that the Large Hadron Collider (LHC) will create the conditions thought to be necessary for time travel. The LHC is designed to probe the mysterious forces that exist at the level of
10   sub-atomic particles, and as such will answer many important questions, such as the true nature of gravity. It is not designed as a time machine.

  In any case, if the LHC became a time machine by accident, the device would exist only at the sub-atomic level so we are not talking about a machine like Dr Who's Tardis, which is able to carry people forwards and backwards from the future.

15   The theoretical possibility is widely debated, but everyone agrees that the practical problems are so immense that it is, in all likelihood, never going to happen. Brian Cox, a Cern researcher at the University of Manchester, points out that even if the laws of physics do not prohibit time travel, that doesn't mean to say it's going to happen, certainly in terms of travelling back in time.

20   'Time travel into the future is absolutely possible; in fact time passes at a different rate in orbit than it does on the ground, and this has to be taken into consideration in order for satellite navigation systems to work. But time travel into the past, although technically allowed in Einstein's theory, will in the opinion of most physicists be ruled out when, and if, we develop a better understanding of the
25   fundamental laws of physics – and that's what the LHC is all about.'

  It comes down to the general theory of relativity devised by Albert Einstein in 1905. It is the best theory we have so far on the nature of space and time and it was Einstein who first formulated the mathematical equations that related both time and space in the form of an entity called 'space-time'. Those equations and the
30   theory itself do not prohibit the idea of time travel, although there have been many attempts since Einstein to prove that travelling back in time is impossible.

  Lots of science fiction writers have had fun with time travel, going back to H.G. Wells, whose book *The Time Machine* was published in 1895 – 10 years before Einstein's general theory of relativity. Interestingly, it was another attempt at
35   science fiction that revived the modern interest in time travel.

  When Carl Sagan, the American astronomer, was writing his 1986 novel *Contact,* he wanted a semi-plausible way of getting round the problem of not being able to travel faster than the speed of light – which would break a fundamental rule of

40 physics. He needed his characters to travel through vast distances in space, so he asked his cosmologist friend Kip Thorne to come up with a possible way of doing it without travelling faster than light.

Thorne suggested that by manipulating black holes it might be possible to create a 'wormhole' through space-time that would allow someone to travel from one part of the Universe to another in an instant. He later realised that this could also in theory
45 be used to travel back in time. It was just a theory of course, and no one has come close to solving the practical problem of manipulating black holes and creating wormholes, but the idea seemed to be sound. It spawned a lot of subsequent interest in wormholes and time travel, hence the latest idea by the two Russian mathematicians.

50 The biggest theoretical problem is known as the time-travel paradox. If someone travels back in time and does something to prevent their own existence, then how can time travel be possible? The classic example is the time traveller who kills his grandfather before his own father is conceived.

The science writer and physicist John Gribbin, who explains these things better than
55 most, has said: 'The snag is that the kind of accidental "time tunnel" that could be produced by the LHC in Geneva would be a tiny wormhole far smaller than an atom, so nothing would be able to go through it. So there won't be any visitors from the future turning up in Geneva just yet. I'd take it all with a pinch of salt, but it certainly isn't completely crazy.'

60 So, not completely crazy, just a bit crazy.

Questions on Passage 1

Marks Code

1. Read lines 1–5.

   (a) Explain why it is that Stephen Hawking feels free to ask if time travel is possible.   **2   U**

   (b) He develops his question about time travel into three further questions. What are they?   **3   U**

   (c) Which word indicates to the reader that one of the questions is of the greatest importance?   **1   A**

2. Explain how physicists look at time (lines 6–7).   **2   U**

3. Show how the writer uses language in lines 15–20 to convey effectively the idea of 'science fiction'.   **4   A**

4. Show how the writer, in lines 15–20 ('Let's indulge ... is not so crazy'), makes the idea about time travel easier to understand.   **3   A/U**

5. Read lines 28–40.

   (a) What is meant by the statement 'where negative energy pulls space and time into the mouth of a tunnel, emerging in another universe'?   **3   U**

   (b) In this paragraph, the writer sets out an argument leading to a conclusion. Summarise the main stages of that argument.   **5   U**

6. Read lines 49–52.

   (a) What is the tone of the final sentence of the paragraph?   **1   A**

   (b) What point does this sentence illustrate?   **2   U**

7. Read lines 53–61.

   Explain what exactly it is that gives cosmologists nightmares.   **2   U**

8. The writer states in line 64 that he believes 'things can't make themselves impossible'. Explain what he means by that remark.   **3   U**

9. How effective is the last sentence as a conclusion to the passage?   **2   A/E**

(33)

Questions on Passage 2   *Marks Code*

10. Read lines 1–11.

    (*a*) What do the Russian mathematicians, Irina Aref'eva and Igor Volovich, believe the Large Hadron Collider near Geneva might create?   **2**   **U**

    (*b*) Why is it that few scientists accept their beliefs?   **2**   **U**

11. Read lines 20–25.

    On what basis does the researcher, Brian Cox, make the claim that 'time travel into the future is absolutely possible'?   **2**   **U**

12. Read lines 36–49.

    (*a*) What revived the modern interest in time travel?   **1**   **U**

    (*b*) Explain how, according to the writer, the theory of 'wormholes' arose.   **2**   **U**

13. How effective is the last sentence as a conclusion to the passage?   **3**   **A/E**

                                                              (12)

Questions on both Passages

14. Which passage is the more effective in sustaining your interest in the possibility of time travel?

    Justify your choice by close reference to both passages.   **5**   **E**

                                                              (5)

                                           Total   **(50)**

Practice Paper G: Higher English

Practice Papers	ENGLISH
For SQA Exams	HIGHER

**Exam G
Critical Essay**

Answer two of the questions

You have 1 hour 30 minutes to complete this paper.

You should answer TWO questions, each chosen from a different section (A–D). You must not choose both questions from the same section.

You may answer each question using texts by Scottish authors.

Make sure that you state the number of the question you are answering in the left hand margin and please take a new page for each answer.

You should divide your time equally between each essay.

The examiners are looking for evidence of the following skills:

- your ability to provide an answer relevant to the question asked and an ability to set out and develop a relevant line of thought

- your knowledge and understanding of the themes and significant, relevant aspects of the chosen texts, as well as your ability to provide detailed, supporting evidence

- your ability to show, where relevant, the ways in which writers' choices of form/structure/language can be used to shape meaning, as well as your ability to provide detailed, supporting evidence

- your ability to evaluate the effectiveness of the text, along with your ability to provide detailed, supporting evidence

- your ability to communicate clearly and accurately, using appropriate written expression.

25 marks are allocated to each question.

SECTION A – DRAMA

Answers in this section should show, where relevant, detailed understanding of the theme(s) of the chosen text and should be appropriately supported by knowledge of relevant dramatic techniques, such as structure, setting, characterisation, dialogue (including, where relevant, soliloquy and monologue), plot, central scenes, climax, dénouement, as well as all relevant aspects of stage instructions, particularly the use of lighting, sound, stage sets...

1. Choose a play in which a main character's internal conflict is a major factor in determining the outcome of the drama.

   Discuss the ways in which the dramatist presents the main character's internal conflict and go on to show how it is used to shape the ending of the play.

2. Choose a play in which hatred is the chief motivating force of one of the characters.

   Show how the dramatist presents the hatred felt by this character and go on to discuss the means by which it forms the motive for his or her actions.

3. Choose a play where the setting is essential in reflecting the main concerns of the play.

   Show how the dramatist establishes the setting and go on to discuss the ways in which he or she uses it to reflect the wider issues of the drama.

4. Choose a play which has at its heart one of the following themes: jealousy, love, revenge.

   Show how the dramatist establishes and develops your chosen theme.

SECTION B – PROSE

Prose Fiction

Answers in this section should show, where relevant, detailed understanding of the theme(s) of the chosen text and should be appropriately supported by knowledge of relevant fiction techniques, such as narrative technique, structure, setting, characterisation, symbolism, dialogue, plot, central scenes, climax, atmosphere, imagery...

5. Choose a **novel** or **short story** which is concerned with unrequited love.

   Describe how the writer establishes the relationship between the characters involved and go on to discuss how the nature of this relationship reflects the wider concerns of the text.

6. Choose a **novel** in which our affection and/or sympathy for the main character is not immediate but develops over the course of the story.

    Show how the main character is presented in such a way that it takes time before we begin to feel affection and/or sympathy for him or her.

7. Choose **two short stories** which explore, in their different ways, the theme of isolation.

    Explain the various techniques by which the writers create and explore the theme of isolation and go on to evaluate which of the stories is the more successful in illuminating the theme for you.

8. Choose a **novel** in which the main character becomes more and more disillusioned about his or her situation.

    Explain what the situation is and go on in more detail to show how the disillusionment is established and further developed.

Prose Non-fiction

Answers in this section should show, where relevant, detailed understanding of the theme(s) of the chosen text and should be appropriately supported by knowledge of relevant non-fiction techniques, such as structure (including sentence structure), narrative technique (including narrative voice), ideas, style, selection of detail, setting, symbolism, use of anecdote and/or evidence, climax, atmosphere, imagery...

9. Choose a **non-fiction text** in which the writer's use of detail makes a convincing impact.

    Show the various techniques by which the writer creates detail and go on to show how his or her use of such detail makes the text all the more convincing for you.

10. Choose a **travel book** with an effective structure.

    Show how the author's use of structure has contributed to the successful impact the book has had on you.

11. Choose a recent (i.e. from this century) **essay or piece of journalism** that deals with poverty and/or prejudice.

    Show the extent to which the author's use of language contributed to the impact the text had on you.

SECTION C – POETRY

Answers in this section should show, where relevant, detailed understanding of the theme(s) of the chosen poem(s) and should be appropriately supported by knowledge of relevant poetic techniques, such as structure (including verse form, rhythm, rhyme), sound, mood, tone, contrast, setting, characterisation, symbolism, synecdoche, climax, atmosphere, imagery, word choice...

12. Choose a poem which takes on increasing significance the more you read it.

    Show how your increased understanding of the techniques used by the poet helped reveal to you the significance of the subject matter of the poem.

13. Choose a poem which presents ideas about communication.

    Show how the poet's use of techniques helps to clarify those ideas for you.

14. Choose **two** poems which deal with the subject of hope.

    Show how the subject matter is established and developed, making clear which of the two poems you find more effective.

15. Choose a poem which explores the ideas of loneliness or separation.

    Show how the poet's use of techniques helps to captivate your interest as he or she explores the ideas.

SECTION D – FILM AND TV DRAMA

Answers in this section should show, where relevant, detailed understanding of the theme(s) of the chosen texts, and should be appropriately supported by knowledge of relevant film and TV drama techniques, such as structure, setting, characterisation, dialogue, plot, symbolism, synecdoche, editing/montage, sound/soundtrack, mis-en-scène (such as lighting, colour, use of camera, costume, props), mood, casting, genre.

16. Choose **a film** or **TV drama*** which presents a difficult subject in a sensitive way.

    Show how the film or programme makers present the difficulties and go on to discuss the ways in which the subject matter was handled sensitively.

17. Choose a **film** or **TV drama*** which uses an unusual method of narration.

    Show how the film or programme makers' exploration of the subject matter benefits from this unusual narrative technique.

18. Choose a **film** or **TV drama*** which portrays a character in conflict with his or her society or community or social group.

    Show how the film or programme makers portray the character and the nature of the conflict, and go on to say how the situation is resolved.

19. Choose a **film** or **TV drama*** which deals with the nature of friendship.

Show how the film or programme makers create character and circumstances that help reveal various aspects of friendship.

*'TV drama' includes a single play, a series, or a serial.

Practice Exam H

Practice Paper H: Higher English

Practice Papers For SQA Exams	ENGLISH HIGHER **Exam H** **Close Reading**

Answer all of the questions

You have 1 hour 45 minutes to complete this paper.

Read the following passages and then answer the questions. Remember to use your own words as much as possible.

The questions ask you to show that you:

understand the ideas and details in the passage – **what the writer has said**
(**U**: Understanding)

can identify the techniques the writer has used to express these ideas – **how it has been said**
(**A**: Analysis)

can comment on how effective the writer has been, using appropriate evidence from the passage –
how well it has been said
(**E**: Evaluation)

The code letters (U, A, E) are next to each question to make sure you know the question's purpose. The number of marks per question will give you a good indication of how long your answer should be.

Leckie×Leckie
Scotland's leading educational publishers

PASSAGE 1

The Sunday Herald leader article, published on 5 September 2010, suggests that we must change our lives, not just our driving habits.

1   In the week that the UK government's chief environment scientist called progress on cuts in greenhouse gases 'an illusion', it would appear from the potential environmental policies being considered by the Scottish government that Holyrood has had enough of illusion and is now pressing for action.

5   The policy document revealed suggests a new aggressive attitude on the environment. It also puts the petrol-driven car centre-stage as one of the contributing culprits to the current failure to meet environmental targets.

There can be little argument that Britain's appetite for agreeing to environmental targets outweighs its delivery record. We sign up to agreements, whether Kyoto or
10   Brussels. We agree to specific dates to meet them. We have also announced we will go further than our promises. But the reality is that targets are not being met. And from the Scottish government's new plans, it is clear they want this regime of drift to change.

Of the 30 or so policies that the administration hopes will make a difference to the
15   pollution affecting Scotland, many are centred on making life far more difficult, and more expensive, for car users. A lowering of speed limits, increased road pricing, higher parking charges and workplace levies are the big stick measures designed to change behaviour. Among the raft of ideas are genuine measures of encouragement, carrots alongside the stick: eco-driving training, grants for low-
20   emission vehicles, investment incentives for low-carbon vehicles, new funding for buses and taxis, incentives to shift freight off our roads. Other agricultural measures, and renewed efforts to bring in new energy technologies, all suggest Holyrood wants to explore all avenues in the bigger environmental picture.

The big question is whether the public will buy into the measures being suggested.
25   Good and brave ideas will come to nothing if they are greeted by an apathetic, or worse antagonistic, electorate. The smoking ban pioneered by Holyrood succeeded because the public had already accepted the need for change and were clear about the benefits. Many of us remain content to pay lip service to the need for action on climate change, even happy to take some small steps towards recycling, but remain
30   hostile to measures which make our lives significantly more difficult. Nowhere is this ambiguity more apparent than in our attitudes to the car.

Most people still do not want to be marched, unwillingly, into accepting green policies. In the current austerity climate, where there is worry over the lack of growth and what this could mean in terms of job losses, the green agenda has
35   suddenly taken a political back seat. It is undoubtedly a brave move by Holyrood to give such a high priority to the environment and to the role of the car at a time when this stance could become a difficult electoral issue. Making motorists pay more is a risky venture, and it will become a political contest if it is openly challenged by opposition parties. There are important issues to be raised if the
40   electorate in Scotland is to be convinced that Holyrood's environmental policy is the result of joined-up rather than blue sky thinking. There is no integrated transport system in Scotland, a scandal for a large and largely unpopulated European

country. Look down any main street in Glasgow and other cities, and you could walk along the roofs of empty buses for hundreds of metres. Do our airports and
45 train stations link in? No. Are cycles given a share of our streets, as they are in Amsterdam? No. Do councils encourage out-of-town shopping complexes where the car is king? Yes. These are competing environmental issues that may first have to be resolved and accepted, to prepare the ground for the lifestyle changes we need to be prepared to make.

50 The harsh reality is that these issues were not dealt with in the boom times and that in an 'age of austerity' they may come too far down personal priorities. There are strong and necessary measures in the government's policy document. The danger is that it becomes a wish list rather than an achievable ambition. To convince the public to take the steps Holyrood will ask of them they need to be
55 convinced those steps are part of a real solution to the environmental crisis.

The big, and still unanswered, question for the environment lobby is how best to manage the cultural change which is the unavoidable logical end to their argument. While welcoming Holyrood's moves to produce specific measures to achieve Scotland's environmental targets, we have to recognise that our politicians have
60 some way to go to persuade the public of our responsibility to change our lives to make them more sustainable. It is in all our interests that they succeed.

PASSAGE 2

Rob Edwards of The Herald *examines the government's plan to cut climate pollution.*

1 Stricter and lower speed limits, higher parking charges and a five pence per kilometre road pricing scheme are being proposed by the Scottish government as part of a major new offensive to cut the pollution that is disrupting the climate. A key policy report reveals that ministers are also considering big increases in
5 spending on walking and cycling, grants for low-carbon cars, and boosts for buses and trains. A further series of radical plans are being drawn up to meet the ambitious target of cutting climate pollution 42% by 2020. These include a renewed £1 billion-plus home insulation scheme, a massive tree-planting programme, bans on dumping waste as landfill, and moves to force farmers to clean up their act.

10 Although the government's new package of 30 'proposals and policies' to combat climate change has been warmly welcomed by environmentalists, some of the measures have already provoked the ire of the car lobby, businesses and farmers. The Association of British Drivers dismissed the curbs on cars as 'lunatic'. They would spark widespread anger, claimed Peter Spinney, the association's co-
15 ordinator in Scotland. 'Whoever brought them in would have to be attempting political suicide,' he said. 'They would be sentenced to a lifetime ban from government.' A specific plan for a £300 a year workplace parking levy has upset the employers' group, the Confederation of British Industry (CBI). 'The fear is that this would be seen as just another tax on business at a time when it can ill-afford extra
20 taxes,' said CBI Scotland's assistant director, David Lonsdale. And farmers are uncomfortable with the suggestion that their public subsidies could be tied to cutting their emissions. These kinds of compulsory measures 'have a bad track record in actually influencing behaviour', according to James Withers, the chief executive of the National Farmers' Union in Scotland.

25   The leaked report accepts that selling some of the policies could be difficult. Increased parking charges are 'unlikely to be widely supported', road pricing is 'complex to deliver' and giving more road space to cyclists is 'likely to face opposition from drivers', it says. But the report argues that the measures it puts forward are 'comprehensive' and 'realistic' options for meeting the climate target.
30   They will enable Scotland's carbon emissions to be reduced from 70 million tonnes in 1990 to 40.6 million tonnes in 2020, it says.

      Dr Richard Dixon, the director of the environmental group World Wildlife Fund (WWF) Scotland, commended ministers for not shying away from tough choices. The proposals would bring widespread benefits, he argued. 'These policies show
35   that tackling climate change can also help solve fuel poverty, reduce accidents on our roads and create a better living for farmers,' he said.

      The Scottish government insisted that one of its budget priorities was a low carbon Scotland. The proposals in the report were options for discussion but may not all end up becoming government policy, it said.

40   For months it has been discussed behind closed doors. It is one of the most important policy documents produced by the Scottish government, and now it has come out of the shadows. The 'proposals and policies' report outlines how ministers plan to meet their ambitious targets to cut climate pollution, all designed to reduce the emissions that are helping to trigger floods, storms and droughts around the
45   world. It is, by any standards, a hugely ambitious venture, that has already garnered many bouquets and brickbats. It gives a taste of the many battles to come, if the government is serious about making Scotland a truly low-carbon economy. There are, for example, plans for 'stricter enforcement' of the 70mph limit on dual carriageways, and to reduce the limit to 60mph on all trunk roads.
50   More 'active traffic management' could include variable speed limits and average speed enforcement.

      On parking, the report assumes a '50% increase' in charges. It suggests that all on-street parking should be controlled by residents' permits and 'pay and display' machines by 2017. However this is 'unlikely to be widely supported except in areas
55   where non-residents compete with residents for limited on-street parking,' it cautions. Similarly, the report proposes a £300 levy on every parking space every year for employers with ten or more staff. It also suggests a nationwide road pricing scheme that would make motorists pay for every trip, linked to the emissions their cars make. This would average out at five pence per kilometre 'on
60   top of existing fuel taxes', the report suggests, but would be 'complex to deliver'.

      The leaked report also suggests a series of more positive policies, including boosting the membership of city car clubs, giving motorists free training in 'eco-driving' and offering £5,000 grants for buyers of low carbon vehicles. There are plans for major investments in improving bus and rail facilities, better travel
65   planning and incentives to shift freight from road to rail and water. Facilities for cyclists and walkers could be brought up to similar standards to those in Sweden, Germany and Belgium, the report says.

Questions on Passage 1

Marks Code

1. Read lines 1–7.

   (*a*) What is the difference in attitude to cuts in greenhouse gases between the UK government and the Scottish government?   2   U

   (*b*) Referring to lines 5–7, how does the policy document regard the 'petrol-driven car'?   2   A

2. (*a*) What evidence does the writer provide in lines 8–13 for claiming that 'Britain's appetite for agreeing to environmental targets outweighs its delivery record'?   3   U

   (*b*) How does the sentence structure of lines 9–11 ('We sign up … are not being met') help emphasise the writer's argument?   2   A

3. Read lines 14–23.

   (*a*) Show how the writer's use of language makes clear what is meant by 'making life difficult, and more expensive, for car owners'.   4   A

   (*b*) Show how the writer's use of imagery in lines 18–23 ('Among the … environmental picture') helps to convey the 'genuine measures of encouragement'. Refer to more than one example in your answer.   4   A

4. Read lines 24–31.

   (*a*) What is meant by the expression 'an apathetic, or worse antagonistic, electorate' (lines 25–26)?   3   U

   (*b*) What reason does the writer give for the success of the smoking ban?   2   U

   (*c*) To what ambiguity is the writer referring when he says 'this ambiguity' in line 31?   4   U

5. Why, according to the writer, has 'the green agenda suddenly taken a political back seat' (lines 33–35)?   3   U

6. Show how the writer's use of sentence structure (lines 44–47) draws attention to Scotland's lack of an integrated transport system (lines 41–43).   2   A

7. What, according to the writer, is 'the big, and still unanswered, question' (lines 56–57)?   2   U

(33)

Questions on Passage 2

Marks Code

8. Explain how the structure of the final sentence of the first paragraph (lines 7–9) highlights what are, in the writer's opinion, the most important proposals to help meet the Scottish government's target of cutting climate pollution 42% by 2010.

3   A

9. Explain how the writer develops his statement that 'some of the measures have already provoked the ire of the car lobby, businesses and farmers' (lines 10 and 12).

3   U

10. Show how the writer's use of word choice in lines 32–36 makes clear his attitude to Dr Richard Dixon's remarks.

2   A

11. Explain what is meant by the expression 'garnered many bouquets and brickbats' (line 46).

2   U

12. How does the writer's use of word choice in the final paragraph (lines 61–67) reinforce the positive policies included in the report?

2   A

(12)

Questions on both Passages

13. Which passage is, for you, the more thought-provoking about the Scottish government's proposals for creating the low-carbon economy?

Justify your choice by close reference to the **ideas of both passages**.

5   U/E

(5)

Total   (50)

Practice Paper H: Higher English

Practice Papers
For SQA Exams

ENGLISH
HIGHER

Exam H
Critical Essay

Answer two of the questions

You have 1 hour 30 minutes to complete this paper.

You should answer TWO questions, each chosen from a different section (A–D). You must not choose both questions from the same section.

You may answer each question using texts by Scottish authors.

Make sure that you state the number of the question you are answering in the left hand margin and please take a new page for each answer.

You should divide your time equally between each essay.

The examiners are looking for evidence of the following skills:

- your ability to provide an answer relevant to the question asked and an ability to set out and develop a relevant line of thought

- your knowledge and understanding of the themes and significant, relevant aspects of the chosen texts, as well as your ability to provide detailed, supporting evidence

- your ability to show, where relevant, the ways in which writers' choices of form/structure/language can be used to shape meaning, as well as your ability to provide detailed, supporting evidence

- your ability to evaluate the effectiveness of the text, along with your ability to provide detailed, supporting evidence

- your ability to communicate clearly and accurately, using appropriate written expression.

25 marks are allocated to each question.

SECTION A – DRAMA

Answers in this section should show, where relevant, detailed understanding of the theme(s) of the chosen text and should be appropriately supported by knowledge of relevant dramatic techniques, such as structure, setting, characterisation, dialogue (including, where relevant, soliloquy and monologue), plot, central scenes, climax, dénouement, as well as all relevant aspects of stage instructions, particularly the use of lighting, sound, stage sets...

1. Choose a play in which a minor character plays an important role.

   Show how the dramatist presents the importance of the minor character and go on to discuss his or her contribution to the outcome of the drama.

2. Choose a play in which the dramatist employs unusual stage techniques.

   Show how some of these techniques are employed and go on to discuss the contribution they make to the success of the play as a whole.

3. Choose a play in which a character is destroyed by the forces within him or her.

   Show how this character's faults are established and go on to show the ways in which they bring about his or her downfall.

4. Choose a play in which the dramatist has created powerfully opposing forces – such as duplicity and honesty or betrayal and loyalty or cruelty and compassion.

   Show how the playwright presents opposing forces and go on to discuss how their resolution contributes to the overall theme of the play.

SECTION B – PROSE

Prose Fiction

Answers in this section should show, where relevant, detailed understanding of the theme(s) of the chosen text and should be appropriately supported by knowledge of relevant fiction techniques, such as narrative technique, structure, setting, characterisation, symbolism, dialogue, plot, central scenes, climax, atmosphere, imagery...

5. Choose a **novel** which deals with a rural setting.

   Show how the novelist develops the setting and go on to discuss how the writer's use of setting provides a suitable environment for the development of one or more than one theme.

6. Choose a **novel** which involves humour.

   Show how the writer has created the humour and go on to show how it contributes to the overall theme.

7. **Short stories**, though interesting in themselves, can also speak truths of a universal nature.

   Show how **two short stories** are both interesting in themselves and are also able to make universal comment.

8. Choose a **novel** which employs an interesting narrative technique.

   Show how the writer uses this narrative technique and go on to discuss what it is about it that interests you.

Prose Non-fiction

Answers in this section should show, where relevant, detailed understanding of the theme(s) of the chosen text and should be appropriately supported by knowledge of relevant non-fiction techniques, such as structure (including sentence structure), narrative technique (including narrative voice), ideas, style, selection of detail, setting, symbolism, use of anecdote and/or evidence, climax, atmosphere, imagery...

9. Choose a work of **non-fiction** that deals with scientific or philosophical issues.

   Show how the writer's method of presenting these issues captured and sustained your interest.

10. Choose a work of **non-fiction** which concerns a world that is different from your own.

    Show how the writer's presentation of that world held your interest despite it being so different.

11. Choose a piece of **non-fiction** which tells the life story of someone whose life is totally different from yours.

    Show how the writer's presentation of that person's life was a factor that made the book interesting for you.

SECTION C – POETRY

Answers in this section should show, where relevant, detailed understanding of the theme(s) of the chosen poem(s) and should be appropriately supported by knowledge of relevant poetic techniques, such as structure (including verse form, rhythm, rhyme), sound, mood, tone, contrast, setting, characterisation, symbolism, synecdoche, climax, atmosphere, imagery, word choice...

12. Choose a poem which depends for its success on its form (poetic and linguistic techniques).

    By close reference to the text, show why the poet's use of form is so important.

13. Choose a poem which deals with an everyday experience.

Show how the poet uses his or her skill to make the everyday nature of the experience revealing to you.

14. Choose a poem which communicates the experiences of loss.

Show how the poet communicates this experience in a way you found meaningful.

15. Poetry can communicate a strong sense of menace.

By comparing **two such poems**, examine the techniques used by the poets to convey an intense sense of menace.

SECTION D – FILM AND TV DRAMA

Answers in this section should show, where relevant, detailed understanding of the theme(s) of the chosen texts, and should be appropriately supported by knowledge of relevant film and TV drama techniques, such as structure, setting, characterisation, dialogue, plot, symbolism, synecdoche, editing/montage, sound/soundtrack, mise en scène (such as lighting, colour, use of camera, costume, props), mood, casting, genre.

16. Choose a **film** or **TV drama*** which is set in the future.

Show how the film or programme makers make clear that it is set in the future and go on to show the extent to which it manages to reveal something about our world today.

17. Choose a **film** or **TV drama*** which portrays historical events in an exciting way.

Show how the film or TV programme makers make the events seem real and exciting to a modern audience.

18. Choose a **film** or **TV drama*** which explores the theme of failure.

Show how the film or TV programme makers use setting and characterisation to explore this theme.

19. Choose a **film** or **TV drama*** where one scene presents a turning point.

Show how the film or TV programme makers build up to the scene and go on to show in detail how the scene brought about change in character and plot.

*'TV drama' includes a single play, a series, or a serial.

Worked Answers

PRACTICE PAPER E   CLOSE READING WORKED ANSWERS

PASSAGE 1

1. (a) The opening question is usually a fairly straightforward one about meaning (U) just to get you started.

> **HINT** There is a kind of Close Reading formula – the first question will concern your understanding of the text and the next will ask about language.

TOP EXAM TIP

It is vitally important, when answering those questions coded **U – understanding**, to use you own words. If you do use the words of the passage you are unlikely to score any marks. **U-coded** questions are there to test your ability to express words, phrases, ideas IN YOUR OWN LANGUAGE.

Answer: In comparison with more sophisticated crime series programmes, *The Bill* is a straightforward, home-spun, uncomplicated (1) series about the everyday work (1) of ordinary policemen and women (1) dealing with the public (1). Any two of these points for 2 marks.

Commentary: As always with Close Reading, make sure you use your common sense – in these opening two lines, *The Bill* is being compared to *CSI, Silent Witness* and *Spooks*, all fairly expensively made, sophisticated programmes, with complex sets involving laboratories and computers, whereas *The Bill* is about the 'bobby' – an ordinary police person 'on the beat', doing his or her everyday job with the public. It's simple and straightforward as opposed to complex and sophisticated.

(b) Now for the language question. Note right away that there are 4 marks available – and that means 1 mark for a simple point, e.g. two simple points about word choice and two straightforward points about sentence structure, or, maybe, two word choice points and one more developed sentence structure point for 2 marks.

> **HINT** The term 'language' covers word choice, sentence structure, tone, imagery, punctuation. Work out which of these you can best use in answering the question.

Answer: Punctuation: the use of the single dash after 'beat' signals an explanation of the preceding statement (1).

Sentence structure: the list following the dash (1) serves to explain in greater detail what is meant by the expression 'bobby on the beat' (1).

Word choice: 'familiar' suggests that the 'bobby on the beat' is well-known, almost a stereotype (1) that the public would know and feel comfortable with (1); 'a little out of date' suggests that its very homeliness, its simple, unpretentious, warm-hearted cosiness, is somewhat out of touch with the modern TV audience's demand for slickness and sophistication (2). Any of the above for 4 marks.

> **HINT** Make sure you improve your vocabulary before May and get practice in expressing ideas in your own words.

Commentary: As well as the above answers, you could always point out that the 'world of DNA fingerprinting' suggests modernity since the world of DNA is a 21st century development; it also suggests advanced police work and a scientific approach to solving crime as opposed to 'bobby on the beat' which suggests mid-20th century approaches to crime prevention. The programmes *CSI, Silent Witness* and *Spooks* are slick and science- and computer-dependent as opposed to the old-fashioned police procedures suggested by the word 'bobby'.

2. (a) 2 marks, therefore a couple of points are sufficient for this (U) question.

> **HINT** The number of marks attached to a question is a clear indication of how much you are required to write and of how many points you need to make.

Answer: In favour of *The Bill,* the writer says (a) that it has endured for more than 25 years (1), and (b) that during all that time it has been the nursery for some very talented actors (1).

Commentary: Sometimes it is useful to enumerate the points you make for the ease of the marker. You could have written that for over 25 years it has been the programme where talented actors have learned their trade. The points are there but not spelled out. Again, you have to make sure that you use your own words in order to get the gist of what is being said.

> **TOP EXAM TIP**
>
> Buy yourself an A6 notebook and use it to jot down the meanings of words with which you are unfamiliar. Use it to build up your vocabulary. What lets many candidates down in this paper is their lack of vocabulary.

> *HINT* ▷ Enumerate or bullet point the main elements of your answer.

(b) With this question (U), make sure you read the paragraph carefully.

Answer: ITV has made a number of attempts to improve the appearance of *The Bill* (1) as well as trying to improve the signature tune (2) (all positive steps even though none worked).

> *HINT* ▷ Remember to put everything that you can into your own words.

Commentary: The term 'series of revamps' suggests changing the look or feel of the programme to improve its appearance or the effect it has on its audience. The 'theme tune' is sometimes referred to as the signature tune – the tune by which some programmes are recognised.

(c) Be aware that you are asked to read lines 4–12. So far the answer has been from lines 4–10 but to answer this question (U) you need to read on.

Answer: ITV avows/maintains that the reasons for ending the programme are (a) mainly artistic (1) since its demise (termination) will mean (b) more funds and assets for plays of outstanding worth (1).

Commentary: The points that you have to explain are 'killed off for creative reasons' and 'high-quality drama' – the marks lie in being able to put those terms into your own words.

3. (a) The word to look out for here is the word 'justifies' – the question is asking you to examine the reasons (therefore a (U) question) he gives for ending the programme.

Answer: He justifies his decision to end the programme on the grounds that changes in TV technology and the styles of programmes have developed, rendering *The Bill* outdated (2); and he also justifies his decision on the grounds that what audiences find acceptable in terms of content and appearance have also altered and developed (2).

Commentary: There are 4 marks available for this question, but if you look closely at what you have to do, you'll see that it is indeed more complex than first appears. The question is asking you to put into your own words the concepts of 'times change' and 'tastes of our audience'. The idea of times changing isn't just the idea that things move on; it is also referring to the notion that, in television, technologies develop and the styles of programmes alter over the years, meaning that an acceptable trend in one decade becomes dated and has to alter by the following decade. He also says that the 'tastes of our audience' change – and 'tastes' here refers not just to what the audience finds acceptable, but to what the audience actually likes, what its expectations are, how far programmes satisfy these expectations.

(b) This question (U) isn't asking you to guess – your answer must be based on the text, typical of (U) questions.

Answer: Because he says that it has been a fixture on TV screens for so long, the real reason is that it has run its course (1); the word 'fixture' in this context has a pejorative connotation, suggesting that it's now dated (1).

> **HINT** ⟩ Don't guess answers – base your answer on the text and on evidence from the text.

Commentary: The director of ITV television makes what appear to be several praiseworthy points about the programme: he says that it has been a 'great institution' – the word 'institution' has, however, a pejorative tone, suggesting something very organisational and confined, ossified and inflexible. It's the same with 'a fixture on our screens for ... 25 years', where the word 'fixture' could mean a date as in a fixture for a cricket match, but, more likely, Fincham means it in the pejorative sense of so fixed in time that it has become dated. He does say that *The Bill* 'has been the home of some of the UK's best serial drama storylines, and a great showcase for scriptwriting and fine acting talent', all of which sounds like a compliment, but he uses the past tense – 'has been', suggesting that those days are past.

Moreover, when he says that in its place there will be 'a wide range of high quality drama' there is the suggestion by implication that *The Bill* is neither high-quality nor drama.

> **HINT** ⟩ Know the meaning of the word 'pejorative' – a tone which is sneering or belittling or insulting. It's a useful word when answering some Close Reading and textual analysis questions.
>
> Know the word 'ossify' – literally to become bone-like, but usually meaning to harden or become fixed and dated.

4. (*a*) Meanings of ideas question (U), the answer to which lies in the text.

Answer: Because each of the characters had his or her personality carefully developed (1) and because the mundane, ordinary work of the police force was made interesting and exciting (1), the programme gained a loyal audience.

Commentary: The answer lies in the sentence: 'The show's rounded characters and ability to find drama in run-of-the-mill police work won a loyal following.' Therefore, what is required is for you to put the two reasons for the loyal following – 'the show's rounded characters' and 'ability to find drama in run-of-the-mill police work' – into your own words. Each reason is worth 1 mark.

(*b*) Language involves word choice, sentence structure, imagery, tone, punctuation, therefore an (A) question – 4 marks means, say, 2 marks for word choice and 2 marks for a developed point about sentence structure, though there are many other permutations.

Answer: Word choice: 'loyal following' suggests a dedicated, devoted audience who faithfully watch the show each week (1); and 'grappling with issues' suggests that thought has gone into the presentation of the complexity of issues such that they are not seen to be cut-and-dried or black-and-white, but are involved and difficult (1, though possibly 2 marks). All this highlights the success of the show.

Sentence structure: the sentence 'Where US cop shows thrived on guns and car chases, *The Bill* focused on muggings and robberies, grappling with issues of racism and social deprivation.' has been inverted (the normal word order would be '*The Bill* focused on muggings and robberies, grappling with issues of racism and social deprivation whereas US cop shows thrived on guns and car chases.') (1, possibly 2 marks). By inverting the sentence, the writer creates a climactic structure with the points about *The Bill* coming at the end and therefore gaining emphasis (1).

Commentary: You could also point out that the way he has structured the last sentence of the paragraph is also climactic, building up to the 'screened three times a week', thus highlighting the success.

> **HINT** ⟩ As with all language questions, pay attention to the task set and make sure you relate the points you make to that task.

5. (*a*) You have to read the first sentence very carefully to find the answer (U).

Answer: The writer makes clear that critics find that *The Bill* has been left behind (1) by more sophisticated US police shows (1).

> HINT You should know the meaning of words such as 'demise'.

Commentary: You need to explain 'critics have found *The Bill* wanting in comparison with complex US police shows such as *The Wire*' – you don't have to know about the US programme called *The Wire* because you can get the gist of the meaning from the idea of the comparison. If *The Bill* is 'wanting' it means that it falls short of or lacks something that clearly the American show has. So the US is making police shows that leave *The Bill* appearing as though it lacks something – presumably sophistication.

(*b*) The answer is in the remainder of the paragraph (U).

Answer: They tried to save the show by going back to hour-long episodes (1) and by killing off some of the main characters (1).

Commentary: The schedulers attempted many strategies: (a) they went back to hour-long episodes; (b) they introduced two fast-moving episodes to run consecutively; (c) they killed off some well-loved characters; (d) they shifted it from the twice weekly 8 o'clock slot to a once a week slot after the watershed – the time after which certain adult action and vocabulary is permitted. There were, then, four major attempts to revive the show but since the question carries only 2 marks, you need mention only two of them.

6. It would seem that you aren't asked to state the tone, but it would be very difficult to answer this question without stating it. The question requires both analysis (A) and evaluation (E).

Answer: The tone used by Heggessey is one of upbeat cheerfulness (1) achieved by words such as 'credit' which has connotations of recognition of a task well done (1) and 'creative high' which suggests that she is convinced the work being done, even at the end, is of artistic merit (1).

Commentary: The tone of her remarks is upbeat and quite cheerful – she says that 'it is a credit' to everyone who has worked on *The Bill*, and the word 'credit' has connotations of thanks and recognition of a job well done; and 'on a creative and editorial high' also suggests that she thinks the programme is performing well, proving itself as a show producing quality drama. You really only need to choose one word and show how it contributes to the overall upbeat tone of cheery thankfulness.

PASSAGE 2

7. (*a*) A meanings of ideas question (U) to get you started.

Answer: The nation valued *The Bill* but didn't hold it close to its collective heart (2).

Commentary: 2 marks are available and right away you can spot that you have to put into your own words the idea that the show was more respected than it was loved. In other words, he feels that *The Bill* was perhaps valued but not necessarily held close to the nation's heart.

(*b*) This time (a clear (A) question) you have to (a) state the writer's attitude, and (b) show how you arrived at your conclusion.

Answer: The writer doesn't think very highly of *The Bill*; he thinks it made very little impact (1) – the fact that it had 'few memorable characters and even fewer memorable storylines' makes clear that he feels that it's instantly forgettable (1). Also, in saying that 'the mourning won't be sustained', he is stating that he feels very few people will miss it after it has ended (1).

Commentary: This isn't a language question as such where you have to analyse word choice, sentence structure, etc. though, of course, you can answer it that way if you want; the best way is to make reference to what is said in order to justify your answer.

Clearly, the writer had a fairly low opinion of *The Bill* – he states that it has 'few memorable characters and even fewer memorable storylines', which leaves little for him to admire. He also says that 'the mourning won't be sustained' for its demise – which makes clear that he thinks very few people will miss it after it has ended. His use of 'Put bluntly' also tells us that he is going to be fairly harsh in his comments.

Were you to make a language comment, a good point would be the structure of the last sentence of the paragraph: note the repetition of the verbs 'went on, held on, kept going' – where the use of anaphora draws attention to the fact that he thinks the programme went on and on, almost mindlessly and unstoppably.

The repetition of 'few memorable' also emphasises his view that it was fairly forgettable. The parenthetical '– like an endurance runner –' also draws attention to his view that the show was 'long-running'.

8. This time (another typical (A) question) you have to make reference to the writer's use of language (word choice, sentence structure, tone, imagery, punctuation) and, though you aren't asked to state his view of the programmes, that has to be implied in your answer. Pay close attention to the task – how does his use of sentence structure *reinforce* his views.

Answer: He regards the programme with contempt, a view supported by the inversion of his first sentence – by placing the subordinate clause at the beginning he delays the main clause, thus building up to the climax, that the programme held its place with 'grim fortitude' (2), an expression which conveys his feeling that the programme is dismal and doesn't deserve its place in the schedules. The repetition of 'the only thing' allows him to expand his view that there was only one good thing about the programme – 'the theme music', which is in a climactic position in the sentence (2).

HINT Be sure always to pay attention to the task and to relate your answer to that task.

Commentary: You can't really help but note that the writer regards *The Bill* as a dismal series: words such as 'grim' make his view that it's dismal stuff fairly unambiguous.

As far as sentence structure is concerned, you should note right away that there are only two sentences in this paragraph and that both have a climactic structure. The writer has inverted the first sentence, placing the subordinate clause at the beginning, thus creating climax by delaying the main clause to the end. But it is his use of 'grim' and 'grindingly' that conveys the deprecating and derogatory nature of his view of the programme. Note also the alliteration of the hard 'g' sound in each word, a guttural sound that conveys an ugliness that supports their meaning and his views.

The second sentence, too, is climactic. The repetition of 'the only thing', when he uses it for the second time, expands his attitude to the theme music. Furthermore, the anaphora reinforces that this is 'the only thing' that he respects about the programme – the theme music – thus implying that, in all other ways, he regards the programme with contempt.

The dash introduces an expansion of his views about the music. And again, in lines 10–11, he uses anaphora: 'As the show quickened, as the plots became louder', repetition that reinforces his disapproval and that builds up to the word 'demented', a pejorative term describing his view about the new theme music.

9. (*a*) This is a meanings of ideas question (U).

Answer: He claims that it isn't a soap because it didn't manage to grip the audience's feelings (1) and it had closed narratives (1), unlike soaps.

Commentary: He claims that it 'didn't make for an involving continuing drama' which is how he defines a soap – therefore for 2 marks you have to put the idea of 'involving continuing drama' into your own words.

(*b*) Again, this is about the meanings of ideas – look at the text and what it says (U).

Answer: Soaps work because people watching can identify and empathise with the characters (1) whose lives make a bond with the lives of viewers (1).

Commentary: He writes: 'Soaps such as *Coronation Street* and *EastEnders* endure because the characters and storylines connect with our emotions.' By '*The Bill*'s characters never imprinted themselves on the primetime psyche' he implies that viewers of primetime soaps are able to identify and empathise with their characters.

10. This (A/E) question is quite difficult but it is worth only 2 marks.

Answer: Any of the points below for 1 mark each.

Commentary: There are several points, worth 1 mark each, that you can make: (a) it's a one sentence paragraph, therefore dramatic and memorable; (b) the 'carriage clock' has connotations of retirement presents, therefore appropriate for a text dealing with the 'retirement' of a programme; (c) the alliteration of 'carriage clock' helps to make it memorable and therefore worthy of a conclusion; (d) a 'carriage clock' retirement gift is a bit of a cliché, appropriate for this programme; (e) it's an old-fashioned kind of gift for an old-fashioned programme, therefore appropriate.

BOTH PASSAGES

11. Note that you are being asked about ideas and not about style, therefore to reach top marks your answer must clearly and convincingly be about the writers' ideas. Also note that what matters isn't the length of your answer but its quality.

Commentary: Avoid simply making a list of straightforward points, but ensure that your answer is (a) grammatically accurate, (b) formal in tone, (c) convincing in its presentation of your understanding of *both* passages, and (d) includes some credible evaluative comment.

In this particular case, though you must deal with both passages, you should concentrate on the passage that presents for you the clearer case for ending *The Bill* and include thoughtful evaluative comment – make clear why you think your choice presents the clearer argument.

The following is a guide to the way marks are awarded:

For 5 marks, you must show that you have clearly and intelligently understood both passages; your evaluative comments must be thoughtful and credible.

For 4 marks, you must show that you have clearly understood both passages; your evaluative comments must be reasonably credible.

For 3 marks, you must show that you have understood both passages; you must attempt evaluative comment.

For 2 marks, you must show that, to some extent, you have understood both passages; you must make at least one relevant evaluative comment.

For 1 mark, you must make one or two comments that may be appropriate but are unconvincing.

For 0 marks, your answer is irrelevant, over-generalised, or mainly lifted from the passages.

PRACTICE PAPER E   CRITICAL ESSAY WORKED ANSWERS

Section A – Drama

1. The word 'climax' can be confusing when it comes to literature. The climax of a play should not be confused with the ending.

Commentary: The climax of a drama is the final point in the play that eventually leads to the ultimate resolution of the conflict and the issues that have been explored. In *Romeo and Juliet*, for example, the climax has to be Juliet's suicide since from that point nothing can get any worse for either protagonist, and in *A Streetcar Named Desire,* the climax has to be the end of scene 10 where Blanche is abused by Stanley.

This question demands close knowledge of the climactic scene, the build-up to it and the consequences of it.

Not only do you need to know which scene is the climax of the play you have studied, but you need to recognise the highly dramatic nature of it. And you must realise that the most dramatic scene in a play is not necessarily the climax. In *Romeo and Juliet*, for example, the scene where Romeo kills Tybalt is highly dramatic but it isn't the climax.

> **TOP EXAM TIP**
>
> Make sure in your preparation for the exam that you know well the beginning of the play, the end of the play, an important central scene AND the climax of the play.

You are asked also to deal with the build-up to the climax – that is, with all that brings the climax about. And you are being asked to say *how* the playwright uses the climax to resolve the issues or themes of the play. The build-up to the climax may take several forms – certainly characterisation, but both setting and symbolism may play an important part. Then, think about how the issues are resolved. Does the death of a main character resolve anything? What, in your opinion, does Juliet's suicide resolve? The end of hatred? Or Willie Loman's suicide? What do you feel resolution and redemption really mean? These terms, and their application to the play you are studying, ought to be thoroughly familiar to you by now. Use the essay to help you come to terms with the structure and working of the play.

2. If you have thought through the use of techniques such as symbolism, then this is the question for you. Even if you haven't begun to think about symbolism yet, then attempting this question now will be an important stage in your study of your chosen play.

> **HINT**
>
> Symbolism can be a powerful way of foreshadowing events in a play (or in a novel for that matter) – symbolism can be anything from a place to a person to an event to an action.

Commentary: Look at the beginning of *A Streetcar Named Desire* by Tennessee Williams and *Death of a Salesman* by Arthur Miller: read carefully the stage instructions of both plays and note the extent to which you should be interpreting the setting in symbolic terms. The names of the cars in *Streetcar* and their destinations, for example, are highly significant. The setting itself is also symbolic, as is the way in which Blanche is dressed. What might be symbolic about Stanley's action in throwing the parcel of red meat to Stella? Look again very carefully at all that is said. In *Death of a Salesman,* read carefully the opening stage instructions and note what is said about the houses and the area.

In *Hamlet*, the opening is about preparations for war and the sighting of a ghost – symbolically significant? But, highly significantly, the wrong guard makes the challenge 'Who's there?' when Bernardo appears for duty – what does that symbolise?

In *Macbeth*, the opening scene is that of the witches with thunder and lightning – given the beliefs of a Jacobean audience, what effect would they have? Do we still regard thunder and lightning as symbolic today? What do we mean by the pathetic fallacy? Look it up on the internet if you're not sure.

3. This question, as you should by now realise, isn't asking about the climactic scene but about a central scene. In Shakespeare, that usually happens in the third act.

> **HINT**
>
> Remember – long before you sit the exam, you should work out which scene in the play you are studying is the central scene. As with everything to do with literary criticism, there is no clear-cut answer: you should work out for yourself which scene you think is central.

Commentary: The central scene is the one which causes some change to take place – either in the plot or in the direction of the play in general or in the protagonist.

Here you have to argue in what way the scene is central or pivotal. In *Hamlet,* some people might want to argue that the scene with Hamlet and the Ghost at the beginning is pivotal in that it sets Hamlet off in a new direction – revenge – but it's perhaps better to think of the scene with the Ghost as catalytic in that it speeds up the reaction. We know already that Hamlet despises his uncle. What about the scene between Hamlet and his mother in her closet (Act III scene iv)? Or even the play scene within the play (Act III scene ii)?

Think about the ways in which your chosen scene is central – does it alter the direction of the plot or the actions of the protagonists? What are the consequences of this scene in terms of the play as a whole? How does it contribute to the resolution of the themes?

4. There is a sense in which the protagonist of any play, particularly a tragedy, undergoes a change – either emotionally (of heart) or in attitude/action/behaviour (of mind).

Commentary: This question is linked to the previous one in that it is usually as a result of the central scene that such a change is undergone. But note, consider *carefully* (a) the build-up to the scene where the change takes place, (b) what happens in the scene, and (c) in what ways the scene caused the protagonist to change, i.e. the outcome of the scene.

The difference between this question and the central scene question is that, here, the focus has to be on the protagonist. In the (a) and (b) part of the above structure, you should be considering the protagonist's role.

Section B – Prose

Prose Fiction

5. These two aspects of the question (a rival's success or a manifestation of the supernatural) are unrelated (though not necessarily), but the latter aspect does allow for those candidates who have studied fiction that deals with the supernatural – *Dracula* is an obvious example, as is *The Woman in Black* by Susan Hill.

Commentary: You will be surprised, when you think about it, how often, in fiction, the protagonist has to deal with a rival's success. An obvious example is *The Great Gatsby* where Jay Gatsby's rival is Tom Buchanan, but there are successful rivals in *Tender is the Night*, *The Cone Gatherers*, *Lord of the Flies* and *Under the Skin*. Just take time to think about the characters in your novel and who may just be a rival.

You then have to consider when the rival's success enters the plot and the ways in which our sympathies for the protagonist are consequently affected.

It's the same with the manifestation of the supernatural: how are our sympathies – especially for Jonathan Harker – affected by the appearance and behaviour of Count Dracula? How about our sympathies for Arthur Kipps when the Woman in Black makes her appearance felt?

6. This is again a question about symbolism and foreshadowing, though directed at fiction this time.

Commentary: The question is asking you to examine the ways in which the setting is established at the beginning of whatever novel you are studying.

Let's take an example. Look at the opening of *The Power and the Glory* – the use of the ether cylinder, 'the blazing Mexican sun and the bleaching dust', the 'few vultures look(ing) down from the roof with shabby indifference', Tench's name and his 'splintering fingernails', then the movement of the vulture as it 'rose and flapped across the town: over the tiny plaza, over the bust of an ex-president, ex-general, ex-human being, over the two stalls which sold mineral water, towards the river and the sea' where it would find nothing since 'the sharks looked after the carrion on that side'.

Look at how well Greene uses setting (all this in one short paragraph) to establish death and to introduce ideas of corruption, shabbiness, the numbing of feelings and pain (the ether cylinder), the possibility of escape suggested by the river and the sea, but there are sharks there. Greene uses setting to establish a run-down, stultifying, death-ridden Mexico during the revolution, a Mexico from which there was no escape except through death itself.

Look equally closely at the novel you are studying – especially at the opening chapter – and work out how the author uses the setting to establish atmosphere and theme.

7. Short stories: the comparative question. This question can be very rewarding to answer, though only if you have been trained in how to do it and have had plenty of practice in essay questions.

Commentary: The idea that fiction (or drama or poetry, for that matter) can add to our understanding of people or society is not an unusual approach to literature in general. Why else do we study literature, but to increase our understanding of the human condition and human experience?

You should consider some of Raymond Carver's short stories, all of which add considerably to our understanding of what it is to be human. Muriel Spark, too, has a number of short stories worth considering.

How have they achieved this understanding? It has to be via setting and characterisation – that's where to begin. But don't deal with one story then the next – compare techniques side-by-side as you develop your argument.

8. This really applies to almost every novel.

Commentary: If a character is going to be a main character, there is a sense in which the reader has to learn more about him/her as the novel progresses. A character who does not develop cannot be a main character – he or she cannot really be very interesting!

But be careful! This particular question is asking you to deal with a character where certain aspects of him/her are *slowly* revealed – and that is not necessarily the case in every novel. One, however, that does spring to mind is *Under the Skin* by Michel Faber.

> **HINT** Make sure that you read the rubric (the wording of the question) very carefully. Failure to do so could cause you to have a lower grade than you expect.

In *Under the Skin*, the narrator takes several chapters to reveal all there is to discover about Isserley, and, indeed, it takes to the end of chapter one to discover an important aspect of her character. It is interestingly done and worthy of being carefully studied. But that could also apply to the novel you are studying – even in *The Cone Gatherers* different aspects of each of the main characters are not revealed instantly.

9. The main characters in many, many novels often display unusual determination.

Commentary: You have to know how that determination is established and developed and go on to show how his/her determination affects your understanding of the novel as a whole – how it affects your understanding of the theme.

> **HINT** 'Your understanding of the novel as a whole' is another way of saying the theme of the novel.

The novel that springs instantly to mind is *The Great Gatsby* – Jay Gatsby shows inordinate determination in his quest for Daisy Buchanan. Look at all that he does: buys a house in West Egg to be near her; throws extravagant parties in the hope of luring her; reaches out to the green light at the end of her dock because it represents his dream of her; arranges for Nick Carraway, the narrator, to set up a meeting with her; and perhaps the greatest show of determination of all is the way in which he re-invented himself when she turned him down the first time. But how does Gatsby's determination affect your understanding of the novel as a whole?

Other main characters have also shown tremendous determination: Simon, in *Lord of the Flies*; Neil, in *The Cone Gatherers*; Isserley, in *Under the Skin*; Arthur Kipps, in *The Woman in Black*. Think how the main character in the novel you are studying has shown determination, then work out how it has been established and developed. Finally, decide how that determination affects your understanding of the novel.

> **HINT** Although most questions refer to 'you', that is merely a way of getting you to identify with the question and find a way into it – when you answer the question, substitute the 'you' with 'the reader'.

Prose Non-fiction

10. The word to pay attention to here is 'striking'.

Commentary: There are several non-fiction texts that depict social values – one of the most obvious being George Orwell's *Marrakech*. You have to say in what ways the text is striking. That means ultimately you have to pay attention to the structure of the piece – the episodic structure where the links aren't chronological or linear but thematic. It's his comments on various aspects of Marrakech's social values, as he saw them, that create the link – the appalling poverty, the injustice, the prejudice, the treatment of women.

But as well as the structure, Orwell's linguistic techniques also make the piece striking – his use of sentence structure, especially climax, and his use of implication – he implies rather than states explicitly and that can be very striking.

11. This is the travel-book-with-a-difference question. It is searching your ability to recognise features of the text other than mere description.

Commentary: Some of the work of Jan Morris and Paul Theroux springs to mind. But what more do such writers accomplish? Social commentary? Politics?

12. Perhaps the best example of this kind of writing is *Stuart: A Life Backwards* by Alexander Masters.

Commentary: Most biographies tend to be about famous people or celebrities, some famous for merely being in the limelight at the time the book is written. *Stuart: A Life Backwards* is an example of a different kind of biography, made memorable by its unusual structure: it begins with the boy as an adult and works backwards through his childhood, looking at the all the causes of his troubled and eventual violent state.

Section C – Poetry

13. It may be that you have studied some satire in class and therefore know about a poem that satirises society. Many 18th century poets, such as Alexander Pope, and 19th century poets, such as Lord Byron, satirised society, and even some 20th century poets such as Philip Larkin and John Betjeman have produced poems that satirise society.

Commentary: Note that you don't actually have to know about the kind of satire involved, but you do have to have a working general knowledge of satire and the way in which it can hold aspects of society up to ridicule. It has to involve humour and the humour really ought to be biting – it's not necessarily the kind of humour that will make you laugh but it will expose some weaknesses concerning human beings and the way they organise and/or exploit their society.

14. Many poems can be regarded as personal – they put into words what you have been thinking. Pope (in the 18th century) put it like this: 'What oft was thought but ne'er so well expressed'. The same applies to feelings – poets have an ability to put the most complex feelings into words.

Commentary: You should take a look at some of Shakespeare's sonnets – he had a profound ability to express the most complex feelings in verse, in sonnet form. A sonnet is a poem comprising 16 lines, made up usually of three quatrains (three four-line verses) with an *a b a b* rhyme scheme, followed by a rhyming couplet at the end, where Shakespeare states a very surprising conclusion to the intricacy of his thinking process.

But there are modern poets who can express thoughts that you will have already had – Seamus Heaney, Ted Hughes, Philip Larkin, Robert Frost and many, many others. Frost's 'The Road Not Taken' would be perfect, since by now you will have thought of the paths that lead to your possible future.

But remember, please, this is not really about *you*. You are writing a Critical Essay about a poem and not a biographical piece about yourself. The feelings are a trigger to launch you into the poem!

15. At least one of the poems you study this year could well be about a character, and one of the best examples of such a poem is Robert Browning's 'My Last Duchess'.

Commentary: Look carefully at the question. A loathsome character? That fits 'My Last Duchess' perfectly, because they don't come much more loathsome than the Duke of Ferrara. But you have also, if you wish, the opportunity to write about someone whom you admire, and Christine Stickland creates a most admirable character in her poem 'Frida Kahlo'.

The structure of both these poems contributes greatly to their success. 'My Last Duchess' is a dramatic monologue, where the Duke is talking to an envoy of his prospective father-in-law about his last duchess and as he does so he reveals, quite unwittingly, the nastiest, downright evil, aspects of his character.

> *HINT*
>
> **Dramatic monologue** – a poem where a speaker addresses an imaginary audience or single speaker using a highly individual register, revealing as he/she does so aspects of his/her personality.

In 'My Last Duchess', for example, as the Duke speaks, there is a changing reaction to his surroundings – he suddenly comments on Neptune, 'which Claus of Innsbruck cast in bronze for (him)'. The envoy's reactions to the Duke's speech are important, but not stated – they can only be inferred from what the Duke says. But it's the unwitting self-revelation of the Duke that makes this poem so successful – he emerges as jealous, acquisitive, greedy, vain and, eventually, murderous.

Perhaps one of the most important techniques used by Browning is his ability to create spoken language – he can capture hesitation and the Duke thinking as he speaks. But most impressive is the hidden rhyme in the poem – it's only after studying it that you realise there is a strict *a a b b* rhyme scheme; it is hidden by the ways in which Browning's use of sentence structure is at variance with the line structure. For example,

> That's my last duchess painted on the wall,
> Looking as if she were alive; I call
> That piece a wonder, now: Fra Pandolf's hands
> Worked busily a day, and there she stands.

If you read the above lines aloud, you won't notice the rhyme. This hidden rhyme captures or suggests the hidden characteristics of the Duke – his nastiness and cruelty.

Another interesting presentation of character is in Carol Ann Duffy's dramatic monologue, 'Stealing', spoken by another fairly unpleasant character – though, this time, one for whom we may feel some sympathy.

On the other hand, Christine Stickland's 'Frida Kahlo', though not a dramatic monologue as such, is nevertheless the presentation of a really admirable character. Much of the success of this poem is due to Stickland's use of contrast and sound.

16. We have just been talking about structure – a dramatic monologue is a precise structure, therefore you could use 'My Last Duchess' or 'Stealing' to answer this question.

Commentary: We have already covered dramatic monologue, but you could also use the sonnet structure to answer this question – one of Shakespeare's sonnets, for example. Sonnet 65 would be an excellent choice – you can talk about the ways in which the structure of the sonnet contributes to its theme of the destructive power of time: by means of the three quatrains, different aspects of time's 'wrackful siege' are explored, while the resolution of the 'battering days' of time comes in the surprising rhyming couplet at the end. It is only then that you realise that it is a love poem – a rather tongue-in-cheek love poem. It is the structure that creates the effects.

Section D – Film and TV Drama

17. Such a question leaves you with a fairly wide choice.

Commentary: You have to do two things – describe the subject involved and then examine the techniques that were used successfully by the film or programme makers. As with literature answers, the 'you' is only to get you involved; as you write, substitute 'the viewer' for 'you'.

But this is really a question about techniques – setting, characterisation, symbolism, and film and television techniques. How are these techniques used to make the subject matter relevant and close to your experience?

18. There are many films and TV programmes that present the dysfunctional family – from the Slaters in Eastenders to the Dursleys in the Harry Potter films; but don't forget that the documentary can also deal with families who have serious problems functioning emotionally.

Commentary: TV has for decades shown an interest in this area – therefore there is a great deal to choose from. You have to concentrate on the ways in which the family or families concerned are presented, but also you have to discuss to what extent the theme(s) involved have been successfully portrayed.

19. Film and TV depend very much on symbolism, which means that you should be able to find something to write about here.

Commentary: When you think about it, a picture of a rose, a still shot in a film of a horse, a slow motion shot of a dancer, are all symbolic – these images are *representations* of the real thing. The photo of the rose is a symbolic image for an actual rose.

Symbolism, then, is hugely important in visual media, such as film and TV – death can, for example, be suggested by the appearance of a vulture. Now think of a film or TV programme that you have studied – how is symbolic imagery used to make the ending resolve the theme?

20. Somebody once said that humour could be more revolutionary than tragedy – here is your chance to deal with comedy that makes a serious point.

Commentary: Comedy in British television and, to a certain extent, in British films, is justly renowned for having a serious undertone which can accentuate serious points. You may well have found yourself laughing at something on TV and then realising that perhaps it wasn't so funny after all. British TV and film-makers are good at using comedy to make audiences think about serious issues. This is your chance to write about such a film or programme or series of programmes.

What you have to do is show how the film or programme makers use humour to make serious comments.

PRACTICE PAPER F — CLOSE READING WORKED ANSWERS

PASSAGE 1

1. (a) This is a 'U' code question and therefore your answer *must* be in your own words.

Answer: The concept of schooling and children learning is in itself a good thing (1) but it has not yet been put into practice (1).

Commentary: Note that Bell doesn't actually define education in these four lines, but he does make clear what it is not. By 'we should try it one day' he implies that we haven't yet tried it, then he goes on to say 'Learning by bitter experience is getting us nowhere' which implies that, perhaps, education should be about learning from experience.

He means, then, that education (schooling, learning) is in itself a good thing, but we haven't yet got round to putting it into practice.

(b) This is a language question (A) and therefore you should look to word choice, sentence structure, tone, imagery and punctuation.

> **HINT** 4 marks means that you need to provide a developed answer which should involve, say, two word choice points and a couple of sentence structure points or a punctuation point and an image deconstructed. A single point, well developed, is worth two marks.

Answer: Punctuation: the dash after the word 'idea' in line 1 signals a throw-away mocking comment (1).

Punctuation: the parenthesis in lines 3 and 4 helps isolate and therefore highlight the additional information 'somewhere, God knows how, or even why', as an irreverent, almost disparaging remark contributing to the mockery (1). Note that we need to keep showing how – *in what way* – the linguistic device helps convey the tone.

Sentence structure: the structure of the parenthetical phrase itself contains the throw-away phrase 'or even why', which, by questioning *why* he has had an education, has the effect of belittling the education itself (2).

> **HINT** You should know about parenthesis – any piece of additional information isolated from the rest of the sentence by paired punctuation marks such as brackets or dashes or even commas. For example, look at the inserted information in line 2 – 'as best I can tell', which is parenthetical, suggesting another throw-away, slightly derisive, almost disrespectful remark, contributing to the mocking tone.

Commentary: First of all, identify the tone – you aren't asked to state what you think the tone is, but it would be very difficult to answer this question without identifying it.

The tone is somewhat facetious, the humour sardonic (mocking). How does he achieve this mocking tone? Unless there is an appropriate word or two that leaps out at you, one that clearly conveys the tone of the first paragraph, then try looking at sentence structure – quite often an analysis of sentence structure is the more useful way of dealing with the task, as is the case here. Also, think about punctuation – there may well be punctuation marks contributing to the effect that you are asked to analyse.

> **HINT** Choose the language features that you know you can deal with best and which are the most appropriate.

Sentence structure: the penultimate sentence is structured as a question: 'But what do I know?' This question is entirely rhetorical – the next sentence doesn't answer it. But the effect is to belittle even more the education that he has had.

2. **(a)** Another U question, worth only 1 mark, therefore the answer doesn't have to be long – it need only make one point, as long as it is derived from the paragraph.

Answer: He thought little of it.

> HINT
>
> When a question appears in an (a), (b), (c) format, be sure to read all the parts of the question before answering (a) – that way, you will save yourself overlap.
>
> If you find that when you move on to (b) you have already covered it, don't waste time repeating yourself. The marker will give you credit in your (a) answer. But try to avoid this by reading all the parts of the question before you begin.

Commentary: We will first of all look carefully at the language used in order to arrive at the answer to (a). Read the fourth sentence very carefully (lines 6–9). Those who survived this older model of education (it was, he says, a kind of Darwinian survival course – i.e. the survival of the fittest) did so because they had 'the knack of feeling well enough' (on the day of the exam) or they were 'resistant to nerves' or they could repeat what they had learned parrot-fashion (i.e. without necessarily understanding it). In other words, he didn't really think very much of his education – it depended on feeling well enough on the day and on being able to regurgitate from memory. The 'truculent parrot' comment suggests that what he had committed to memory didn't have to be understood – and that is fairly damning.

(b) Some language questions (A) attract 4 marks, often where the article is particularly rich in linguistic features, such as this article.

> **TOP EXAM TIP**
>
> If you know about adverbs you will find some language questions easier to answer. Adverbs are words which modify or add to the meaning of (usually) verbs. For example, he crossed the road *slowly*, where *slowly* tells the reader *how* he crossed the road.

Answer: Word choice: 'Darwinian survival course' is a hyperbole – to regard education/exams as a matter of the survival of the physical and emotional fittest is to mock by gross exaggeration (1).

Word choice: to compare an examinee to a 'truculent parrot' is to mock the person and the whole education system that has exams as tests of knowledge (1).

Sentence structure: The fourth sentence is in the form of a list, the effect of which is to delay the final punchline – 'You may turn over your paper' – as long as possible, building up to and creating a climax: the moment when examinees are faced with the test of all their education. And therein lies the mockery of his comments – that sitting an exam should be the test of being educated (2).

> HINT
>
> 'Language' means examining sentence structure, word choice, tone, imagery and punctuation.

Commentary: Sentence structure: there are two short opening sentences which build up climactically to a third longer sentence. The third sentence contains the humour achieved by the switch in preposition from swear *by* (meaning to put your trust in something) to swear *at* (meaning to be annoyed by something). So his education is something that some people admire and trust but that he realises was worthless and annoying because so many people were let down by the system – therefore he would swear at it. But there is the climactic build-up to the 'swear at it' which helps intensify the mockery and the humour.

Similarly, the long fourth sentence is also climactic – the build-up achieved by the parenthetical 'poor souls' and the list of adverbial phrases ('on a kind of Darwinian survival course shaped around the knack of feeling well enough', 'resistant to nerves', and 'with all the easy fluency of a truculent parrot', 'at the moment someone said') all modifying the verbs 'chewed up and spat out'. This list delays the final punchline 'You may turn over your paper' – the moment when examinees are faced with the test of all their education. And therein lies the mockery of his comments – that sitting an exam should be the test of being educated.

You could also comment on the punctuation – by using as strong a punctuation mark as a colon to introduce 'You may turn over your paper' he isolates the expression and therefore makes the mocking tone clear. You could make this same point under tone!

Word choice: 'Darwinian survival course' is a hyperbole in that regarding education as a matter of the survival of the fittest is mockingly exaggerated.

Word choice: to compare an examinee to a 'truculent parrot' is to mock the person and the whole education system that has exams as tests of knowledge. The word 'truculent', suggesting rudeness and even aggression, adds to the mockery.

3. A U-coded question, the answer to which is there to be found in the text and put into your own words.

Answer: He knew he could successfully cram enough knowledge for a couple of weeks before an exam (1) and that was better than studying all year round (1) and better than leaving school and taking a job (1).

Commentary: You are asked to give the writer's reasons for liking exams. Read the paragraph (lines 10–14) carefully. He says that his preference is for 'vacuum-packing (his) head for a fortnight prior to a quiz' – i.e. he prefers to cram before an exam. He goes on to say that cramming 'was better than working' and better than studying all year round. There we have his reasons for liking exams.

4. This question demands both analysis and evaluation: you have to say for 3 marks the ways in which 'The real test was how to handle the test' is an effective conclusion to the paragraph.

Answer: The sentence is short and aphoristic, therefore memorable (1); it repeats the word 'test', not only highlighting it – the paragraph is about tests and exams – but also drawing attention to the two meanings of the word as used here – (a test as in an exam and a test as in being able to cope with the exam successfully) (2).

HINT
> Know the words aphorism (short, neat expression, like a saying) and succinct (something concise and to the point). Such vocabulary enables you to answer questions quickly and effectively.

Commentary: Use your common sense about conclusions – they must in some way *conclude* – i.e. sum up what the paragraph is about. Look for ways in which the sentence does that, but also look for illustrative material or memorable phrases. Here, the neatness of the sentence, the way in which it repeats the word 'test', its aphoristic rhythm, all go to make it memorable and therefore effective. Short phrases or sentences that have a ring to them make good conclusions.

But more than that, look at what the paragraph is about. The 'test' should have been the exam itself, but since the pupils could anticipate the questions ('the exam-setter ... persisted with the Shakespeare question *some of us always knew was coming*'), it wasn't really a test. The test was to know how to con the system by working out what the test would be about – i.e. by coping with the test such that you could pass it.

5. (*a*) Put the sentence into your own words (typical of U questions).

Answer: He means that by succeeding in achieving a degree from the university, he had once more conned the system (1) but this time the 'royally' signals that he had conned it at the highest level (1).

Commentary: The phrase 'patting my head at the University of Edinburgh' is a reference to receiving his degree (at a graduation ceremony, the principal or whoever touches your head and declares that you have been made Master of Arts or a Bachelor of Science or whatever is the title of your degree); he maintains that all his graduation meant was that he had got away with it – he had conned the system once more, only, since it was at degree level, he had got away with it *royally* – he had got away with it big time.

(b) This is an A question, and although you aren't asked what it is he thinks education should involve, nevertheless it's easier to answer the question if you do answer this.

Answer: The structure of the following sentences – 'But educated? Equipped? Rounded?' – is in the form of questions which reveal that he believes that the individual should be properly educated, prepared to deal with the world, and have a rounded view of things. These questions are rhetorical – the negative answer is clearly implied (2). Moreover, the fact that all three are minor sentences draws attention to their meaning – that the current system fails to achieve any of these goals (1).

> **HINT** A minor sentence is a sentence without a finite verb – that is, a main verb, a verb that shows both tense and person. Minor sentences can contain non-finite verbs.

Commentary: You have already got a fairly clear indication by now of what he thinks education should involve – he has already said that 'real learning for its own sake' (line 21) took place 'well away from school'. He thinks that education should involve real learning – making the learner independent and able to think for him or herself.

The sentence structure highlights his views by the use of the three questions – 'But educated? Equipped? Rounded?' They reveal that he believes that the individual should be properly educated, prepared to deal with the world, and have a rounded view of things. The fact that all three are minor sentences draws attention to their meaning. The following sentence is also a question – suggesting that the current system qualifies you only to pass exams, not to think for yourself.

(c) Questions about imagery are A questions, and do remember to give the literal meaning of the image you choose.

Answer: In 'it's a very small return in an investment made' the writer draws on the imagery of the finance industry, suggesting that for all the cost (in terms of effort and in setting up the country's entire educational system) his ability to answer the occasional arts question on *University Challenge* isn't a huge gain, a huge benefit to him or to society at large (2).

Another way of answering this would be: just as people invest in a company in order to get a return on their money (or indeed get little return despite their investment), so everything that both he and the country as a whole put into the educational system has not produced many benefits (2).

Both the above are worth 2 marks.

Commentary: There are several images in these lines – farming imagery ('chaff', 'to waste like crops', 'threshing'); imagery of demolition ('debris'); medical imagery ('coma'); financial imagery ('small return' and 'investment'); gambling ('odds were slashed'). Choose the image that you can handle best and allows you to write most.

6. You need to recognise this as the link question (A).

> **HINT** Questions about structure are invariably link questions – the answer to such questions has to do with the way the sentence (or paragraph) acts as a link in the argument.

Answer: The expression performs a linking function (1), linking what he has said in the previous paragraph to this paragraph. The word 'answer' refers back to the last sentence of the previous paragraph 'And why?' (1) and the answer to why chances were ruined is signalled by the colon (1) indicating the list of reasons.

Commentary: The word 'answer' obviously refers back to the question which forms the last sentence of the previous paragraph – 'And why?' – the answer to which is signposted by the expression 'is straightforward' and further indicated by the colon. After the colon comes the actual answer – 'Screw this up and ...'.

7. A question, coded U, which asks you to list the consequences brought about by the educational system we have in place.

Answer: Although we recognise as a society that there is a need to reform our schools (1), we are not sure what the nature of that reform should be (1) and hence we are unable to get round to putting it into place (1).

Commentary: The answer to the question comes in the previous sentence and is signalled by the word 'this' – a demonstrative adjective that has, as its antecedent, all the consequences we need to pinpoint: that while we recognise the need to reform the system, we are failing in that we cannot make up our minds about what we want from our schools. Moreover, we cannot seem to get round to organising the very reform that we think ought to take place.

PASSAGE 2

8. 'How effective?' questions involve evaluation on your part (E) and you can answer that you do or do not find (in this case) the anecdote effective. Or you can say you find it partially effective. The marks are awarded for the extent to which you justify your view, and that requires some analysis (A).

> **TOP EXAM TIP**
>
> Find out from the internet or your teacher what is meant by a demonstrative adjective and an antecedent adjective.

Answer: In lines 6–8 the anecdote effectively illustrates and makes clear the writer's view that older people are liable to benefit more from academic education (1). He states that he 'might have learned' much more 'from this fine scholar' had he 'just been a bit older' – from which we can infer that he means that more mature people might benefit more from education than those who have just left school.

Commentary: When the writer reflects on how much more he 'might have learned from this fine scholar if (he) had just been a bit older, a bit more mature', he is suggesting that education may benefit more mature people more than those who have just left school. Since the anecdote makes that view clear, it is effective.

9. (a) This is a U-coded question, requiring the answer in your own words.

Answer: Primary education is important because it helps those pupils who are underprivilaged (1) at the earliest stage of the education process (1).

Commentary: The answer lies in the lines 'This is where priority investment is essential; this is where we must help those who are already disadvantaged, even before they have started properly on life's long journey.'

There are 2 marks available – but you can see that he makes two points about the importance of primary education – you just need to put the points into your own words.

(b) Again a U-coded question worth 2 marks.

Answer: What most affects a child's ability to do well at school is his home background (1) and parental feelings towards the school (1).

Commentary: He says in lines 23–27 that the biggest influence on a pupil's progress at school surely remains their domestic background and parental attitudes about education – 2 points for 1 mark each, but they have to be in your own words.

(c) This kind of question is really asking you to look at the language to say how something has been developed – pick up on words/expressions that develop the idea asked about. But since it is about your understanding of ideas, the question is coded U.

Answer: Those who perform well at school have parents who are encouraging and helpful (1); they also have room and peace in order to study (1); whereas those who underperform educationally have neither of these basics for study – to have encouraging parents and peace and room to work belong for them in the realms of fantasy (2).

Commentary: This time the explanation of what is meant comes after the phrase given in the question – after he mentions the acute disparities in young children's home backgrounds he goes on to say: 'Many children go on to do well at school if they come from somewhere where education is valued, where the parent or parents are supportive, and where there is at least a modicum of space and quiet for study'. For too many youngsters in SQA country, however, such simple requirements remain a utopian fantasy'. The language is quite difficult but if you break it down he is really making three points – children who do well at school have supportive parents (1st point) and have a quiet place to study (2nd point), whereas for far too many pupils such things are not just out-of-the question but are in the realms of fantasy (3rd point). Now all you have to do is couch those three points in your own words.

10.   Again the answer lies clearly in the text – and has to be put into your own words (U).

Answer: If we educated people properly, there would be less need for such high spending on social services (1) and more could be devoted to education since social services would require less (1).

Commentary: He states clearly how we achieve an ideal world: 'In an ideal world, we would spend at least as much on education as on the social services. But how do we try to achieve an ideal world? Through education.' But be careful – the answer isn't just 'Through education'; it involves spending at least as much on education as we do on social services, and the only way we can do that is if we educate properly and have fewer people in need of social services.

11.   Questions that use the expression 'to what extent' can be answered by saying 'yes' or 'no' or 'yes and no'! but such questions require both analysis (A) and evaluation (E).

Answer: The anecdote about Keir Hardie is an effective way of ending the passage because it illustrates the writer's points about the great importance of education (1) and also it illustrates how lucky children are today to have education made available to all (1). It captures the idea that some children – i.e. the writer and his fellow pupils – are born very lucky in being able to take advantage of the education on offer (1). Each of the above for 1 mark.

Commentary: You could argue that the anecdote undermines his argument – which is based on academic achievement being dependent on home circumstances; the anecdote seems to suggest that if more children were like Keir Hardie then more would overcome the difficulties to succeed educationally. On the other hand, you could argue that it is effective because it draws attention to the importance of education and that, nowadays, with education for everybody available 'free', it should be appreciated more. Or you could argue a combination of the positive benefits of this anecdote with the negative ones.

BOTH PASSAGES

12.   Note that you are being asked about ideas – which of the passages provides the most thought-provoking ideas about education. Base your answer on *both* passages but concentrate on the one which, for you, presents the better, more thoughtful case concerning ideas about education.

Commentary: What matters isn't the length of your answer but its quality. Avoid simply making a list of straightforward points, but ensure that your answer is (a) grammatically accurate, (b) formal in tone, (c) convincing in its presentation of your understanding of *both* passages, and (d) includes some credible evaluative comment.

See question 11 on page 72 for a guide to the marking criteria.

> **HINT**   It's probably best to choose the passage about which you can write the more convincingly, but include both passages.

<hr>

PRACTICE PAPER F   CRITICAL ESSAY WORKED ANSWERS

Section A – Drama

1.   Someone once wrote that the most interesting characters in Shakespeare's plays are his villains and, in a sense, this question is getting at that idea. Certainly this could apply to Iago (*Othello*), Macbeth (*Macbeth*), Claudius (*Hamlet*), Edmund, Goneril, Regan (*King Lear*).

Commentary: To answer this question you have to ask yourself: do any of the villainous characters have redeeming qualities that could engage the audience's sympathies? Take Macbeth, the eponymous villain of *Macbeth*.

> **HINT**   'Eponymous' means that the title of a play has the same name as one of the characters.

Macbeth, you may think, is one of Shakespeare's worst, most evil, villains. Not only does he kill a king (regicide), but he has his colleague and friend, Banquo, murdered and, almost worse still, he has Macduff's wife and child murdered – somehow the killing of women and innocent children seems utterly unforgivable. It would appear the man has no redeeming features. Yet, towards the end of the play, after his wife's suicide, he recognises that nothing that he has done has been worth it. He sees life as: 'a tale/Told by an idiot, full of sound and fury/Signifying nothing'. He had massive ambition, became King of Scotland, yet in his latter years he realises that it hasn't been worth it – life is about nothing – no thing – it is utterly vacuous. He also says elsewhere, when talking of growing old:

> And that which should accompany old age,
> As honour, love, obedience, troops of friends,
> I must not look to have, but in their stead
> Curses, not loud but deep, mouth-honour, breath
> Which the poor heart would fain deny and dare not.

He is lamenting the fact that in his old age, because of all that he has done, he cannot expect to have 'honour, love, obedience, troops of friends': he has lost the respect and affection of others; he has no friends. He can hear 'curses, not loud but deep': people curse him but not to his face. He has only 'mouth-honour': his courtiers pay him lip-service, they say they honour him but it is not meant. It would seem that Macbeth regrets what he has done because now he recognises the consequences of his actions – that can engender some sympathy.

But maybe, more than that, there is something admirable about Macbeth at the end. When Macbeth is told that Birnam wood is coming to Dunsinane, he realises that the weird sisters were 'the fiend / That lies like truth' and that he could now die. But rather than act cowardly he declares:

> Ring the alarum bell! Blow wind, come wrack;
> At least we'll die with harness on our back.

He shows great bravery and fortitude in the face of certain attack and probable death – and these are the actions of a man for whom we can feel some sympathy.

You see that you have to argue your case. If you have studied, say, *Othello*, do you think Iago has any redeeming features? Is there any way you can feel some sympathy for him?

But what if your play isn't by Shakespeare, but by Arthur Miller? Are there villains in *Death of a Salesman* or *A View from the Bridge* or *The Crucible*? Eddie Carbone is probably the only character who comes close to being villainous and would be a good choice for this question.

2. Again, a Shakespearean tragedy would seem a better choice for this question than a modern drama. Certainly, *Macbeth* and *Hamlet* have comic elements – *Macbeth* has the porter's scene with its jokes about drunkenness and *Hamlet* has the gravediggers' scene with its jokes about death.

    The question you have to ask yourself is whether these humorous scenes in these plays enhance the tragedy or detract from it? There is such a term as 'black humour' – humour that is juxtaposed with tragic elements.

HINT ▷ Learn how to spell 'humorous' – it's worrying how many candidates spell it wrongly.

Commentary: Black humour often implies a comment, the effect of which is highly disturbing. For example, the wit in the gravediggers' scene in *Hamlet* can, maybe, cause us to laugh and, then, we pause and wonder what we are laughing at – human beings don't really regard death as funny or even as the subject of wit. Therefore, when one of the gravediggers almost accidentally makes jokes about his trade – he thinks he is being serious – we can laugh at his misconceptions, then realise that what we are laughing at isn't really that amusing. Wit or humour can, if juxtaposed with tragic material, actually highlight the gravity of it.

HINT ▷ Learn the meaning of the word 'juxtaposed': it merely means side-by-side. It does *not* mean a contrast or even imply a contrast.

3. Obviously, it would be wise to choose a play the ending of which you know well. Most plays that you study will, to all intents and purposes, have endings that are satisfactory.

The Shakespeare plays that you are likely to study have satisfactory endings, all of which are to do with retribution and/or redemption. It's often said of Shakespearean characters – and maybe of all dramatic characters – that the good are rewarded and the evil get their just deserts. Is this true of the play(s) you have read in class?

Commentary: Aristotle (384–322 BC), a Greek philosopher and critic, talked about catharsis – a cleansing or purification of emotions that should take place at the end of a tragedy. The death of the protagonist (hero or main character who is part of the forces for good) is acceptable because it brings about feelings of sorrow, pity, a release from pent-up emotion. This great pity is felt by the other characters in the play but, perhaps even more importantly, it is felt by the audience. Sometimes you get a real feeling of waste – it's a waste that Hamlet had to die and a lesser person – Fortinbras – take over. It's a waste, but at least the build-up of tension has been released and stability has returned.

Even in the case of Macbeth – a brutal tyrant – at the end there is a feeling of waste: that it could have been otherwise. He was brave, determined, intelligent, and in his way heroic (in the beginning and at the end). He had king-like qualities which he put to appalling use – and his death meant the tremendous release for the other characters and for Scotland. But, and maybe it is a small 'but', his death brings about in some of the audience a feeling of waste as well. It cannot of course be denied that his death is retributive; but it is also redemptive in that Scotland is rescued from its tragic decline and corrupt state. Malcolm is now king and stability has returned – but so has ordinariness.

What about Eddie Carbone's demise? To what extent is his death retributive? Is it redemptive? Does it bring about stability again? Is there any sense of its being a waste? Is the ending satisfactory?

What about Blanche DuBois in *A Streetcar Named Desire*? Although she doesn't die as such, nevertheless she is rejected by her society. The old-fashioned values represented by Blanche are contained and destroyed by the new, materialistic values of modern 20th century America – values represented by Stanley Kowalski.

Although we may regret some of the endings of these plays, that's not what the question is asking – you have to consider the extent to which the endings are *satisfactory*. Are they fitting in terms of the play and its themes?

Ask yourself these questions about the ending of the play you have studied.

4. This isn't so much a question about realism in drama, though it could be about that. You could argue that though Miller and Williams are modernist playwrights using non-realist sets and techniques, nevertheless they face reality in ways which earlier, more realistic, plays didn't.

But you can also take this question more literally and examine the extent to which characters face challenges. Look at the second sentence of the question for clarification.

Commentary: What challenges does Miller present his characters with? Is Eddie Carbone's challenge his own jealousy? Is it his over-developed affection for his niece? Is he facing the challenge of his own latent homosexuality? Is it his inability to see beyond his clichéd notion of masculinity?

And what challenges is John Proctor faced with? His loyalty to his wife undermined by his lust for Abigail? And what of Willy Loman? Is the challenge that he faces the challenge of a changing America that no longer values people and their sense of loyalty?

Make sure that you think these things through before you answer the question. Make sure you know what challenges are faced by the main character of the play you have studied, but, even more importantly, make sure that you know how that character deals with the challenges.

Section B – Prose

Prose Fiction

5. Perhaps it would be best here to make clear how you choose to interpret the word 'affair'. The word can mean a relationship between two people who are not married to each other. But that is a fairly narrow interpretation of the word for the sake of this essay – it would restrict, for example, the characters you might want to discuss in *Tender is the Night* to Rosemary and Dick Diver. In this sense the word 'affair' has a pejorative feel to it; it suggests a relationship which is not really acceptable within our social mores.

> *HINT*   'Mores' is another word for customs or social standards.

But if you take the term to mean two people who are in love with each other, then more characters spring to mind. It would be best to make clear your own interpretation at the beginning of your essay.

Commentary: Perhaps not that many novels with the theme of a love affair which has ended spring quickly to mind, though *The Great Gatsby* and *Tender is the Night* certainly do. Both novels deal with more than one ended love affair: in *The Great Gatsby* there is obviously the affair between Daisy and Gatsby that ended five years previously, but there is also the brief affair between Nick Carraway and Jordan Baker. In *Tender is the Night*, the obvious choice is Dick Diver and Nicole Warren, who actually marry but it doesn't last very long. There is the affair between Abe and Mary North – but that ends with Abe's death in New York.

The question goes on to ask you how our sympathies for the characters are affected by the ways in which the situation is resolved. You need, therefore, to be certain of what happened, how the affair ended, and how our sympathy for each of the characters was affected by the ways in which it ended. How did the affair between Daisy and Gatsby end? Who ended it and why? And how are our sympathies affected by the way in which it ended? In a very real sense that is why Gatsby re-made himself and certainly why he decided to become rich. What about Daisy? The girl with the voice full of money?

6. Many novels deal with journeys, but once more you need to be able to see/understand the metaphorical aspect of the journey.

Commentary: Perhaps the novel that springs most readily to mind is Joseph Conrad's *The Heart of Darkness*, in which the reader is told the story of Marlow's journey from the Thames to the Congo and thence upstream to meet Kurtz. The journey itself is the journey into the heart of darkness and both rivers, the Thames and the Congo, take on metaphorical significance.

But other novels involve a journey – Ishiguro's *The Remains of the Day*, Cormac McCarthy's *The Road* and even Greene's *The Power and the Glory*.

> *HINT*   Be prepared to see a journey as metaphorical – the journey through life, for example.

7. The short story question. You are asked about the comment on human nature made by the short stories – and you have to go on to say which is the more successful at clarifying some aspect of people or society.

Commentary: All literature, in a sense, makes a comment on the human condition and all short stories make some kind of comment on people or society. For example, *The Verger* by Somerset Maugham says something about dignity and adaptability, while *The Natives are Hostile* by Alistair Scobie says something about survival. If you are preparing for the short story question in the Higher – a dangerous strategy if that's all you are preparing for the fiction section – then you must be certain of the theme is of each of the stories that you are studying.

> **HINT** Make sure in your preparations for the fiction section that you study more than just short stories.

Be sure that you know the themes portrayed and that you know the various techniques used by each short story writer. You need to be able to refer to everything in detail and you need to be able to make a point-by-point comparison.

8. The question is asking you to consider what surprising aspects of the main character are revealed in the novel. It would be advisable to define what you understand by the word 'surprising' or be able to say in what ways the character displays surprising aspects of his or her character.

Now read carefully what you have to do: you have to make clear the ways in which the writer achieves this revelation – in other words, how is it done, how is it portrayed/presented? Then you have to show how the revelation affects the reader's opinion of the character.

Commentary: For example, in *Under the Skin* by Michel Faber, the narrator reveals to us some very surprising aspects concerning Isserley's physical appearance and behaviour. The writer achieves this revelation by using the narrator to reveal these aspects gradually – the first strange aspect of her behaviour is not revealed until the end of Chapter One. Thereafter, gradually, we discover more and more aspects of her that are really very surprising.

Interestingly, the writer of *The Great Gatsby* chooses a different way to reveal surprising aspects of the character of Gatsby. He uses the narrator, this time a character in the novel, one Nick Carraway, to reveal these aspects using flashback (or analepsis). We discover various surprising aspects concerning him by means of conversations with other characters and conversations with Gatsby himself as he tells Nick about the past. You need to work out what the surprising aspects are.

Prose Non-fiction

9. The question is about structure – how has the writer used structure in order to engage the reader's attention?

> **HINT** When preparing your work for the Critical Essay, think along the lines as set out on pages 8–9. Note the importance always of structure.
>
> Structure is about time – beginning > middle > end. Sometimes time can be presented in linear structure and sometimes the narrative structure is episodic.

Commentary: It is because of the structure of *Shooting an Elephant* by George Orwell that the reader's attention is arrested and held. He begins with the account of shooting the elephant which is gripping in its detail – that's what grabs our attention. But then Orwell, having engaged the reader's attention, is able to go on and reflect on the nature of authority and of Empire.

> **HINT** In non-fiction answers, candidates can only too easily fall into the trap of dealing with what the essay or piece is *about*. For example, when it comes to biography don't fall into the trap of dealing with the person – deal with the ways in which the writer has presented the person.

10. Here is your opportunity to write about an essay written in an earlier century: since it doesn't say earlier than which century, you can take it that anything written in the 20th century is acceptable – and again Orwell's essays are perfectly acceptable. But it does mean that material written by Melanie Reid or Ian Bell or Ruth Wishart in this century is unacceptable.

Of course, if you have read any essays by Joseph Addison or Richard Steele then those also are acceptable, as they were written in the early part of the 18th century when the last Stuart monarch was on the throne.

Commentary: The important aspect of this question is to show how the presentation of material by the writer makes it as relevant, as a commentary, on today's social issues. Orwell's essays certainly do that, as do some of Addison's and Steele's.

11.   This time it's the language of travel writing and the ways in which it captivates and engages the reader's interest.

Commentary: It is perhaps worth reading *As I Walked Out One Midsummer Morning* by Laurie Lee – his account of arriving and traveling throughout Spain are made absorbing because of his use of language. The account of his arrival in Spain is a delight to read.

Section C – Poetry

12.   You have probably been taught a number of love poems, and some of the most effective are among Shakespeare's sonnets.

Commentary: The sonnet is very much a format that we associate with love poetry. There are two very recognisable sonnets – the Petrarchan or Italian sonnet of 8 lines followed by 6 lines (14 in all) and the Shakespearean sonnet (three 4 line verses, followed by a rhyming couplet). Look at Sonnet 18 by Shakespeare – 'Shall I compare thee to a summer's day?', the first two quatrains of which are a description of summer, followed by what is referred to as the volta – the change or switch in direction. The volta is at the beginning of the third quatrain and heralds the shift from Shakespeare's generalised comments about the temporary nature of summer to the particular comment concerning the ways in which his lover is 'eternal summer', whose beauty 'shall not fade'. The poem ends with the rhyming couplet that surprises us by its comment that as long as this sonnet survives so shall his lover. And of course, the sonnet has survived!

There are many love poems by other poets. But it might be worth looking at 'Modern Love' by George Meredith. For a 19th century poem, it is remarkably apt.

13.   Ambiguity – the stuff of poetry! How many ambiguous titles of poems do you know?

Commentary: One poem which most effectively exploits ambiguity is 'Midterm Break' by Seamus Heaney. The very first line of this poem exploits ambiguity. It states: 'I sat all morning in the college sick bay' which instantly suggests that the persona is too ill to attend classes, an impression furthered by the following line, 'Counting bells knelling classes to a close', which suggests that he is passing the time by counting chimes of the bell. It's not till later that we realise that he is at boarding school and is waiting to be taken home for his little brother's funeral. It's only then we realise that the word 'knelling' is ambiguous, not merely describing the sound of a bell being rung slowly but the sound of a bell associated with death and funerals. The poem goes on, its real meaning slowly revealed, as the reader realises that some of the images are ambiguous and have another, more solemn, meaning.

HINT ▷ The narrator of a poem is often referred to as the persona – that way we avoid making the assumption that the poem is being narrated by the poet.

Look carefully at the poems you have studied and see if you can work out the extent to which they are ambiguous.

14.   Probably every pupil in every school studies war poetry. This is often thought to be more suitable for pupils in fourth year, but that isn't necessarily the case.

Commentary: Some of Wilfred Owen's poetry – 'Miners', 'Strange Meeting', 'Exposure' – are very subtle, requiring mature minds. Also, 'Break of Day in the Trenches' by Isaac Rosenberg is a war poem worthy of serious study. Be sure, however, to deal with war poems in depth.

15.   The question about the comparison of poems really ought to be avoided unless you have been taught *how* to compare poems. Here you are asked to compare two poems that are the result of reflections on intense emotional experiences. But the question is to compare the ways in which the poets have conveyed the *intensity* of the experiences, which means you are looking for powerful imagery and other poetic and linguistic techniques.

Commentary: Some of the poetry of Ted Hughes undoubtedly communicates intense emotional experiences, as does the poetry of Tony Harrison. Perhaps with this question it would be better to compare two poems by the same poet.

Section D – Film and TV Drama

16. There are many, many films and TV dramas which deal with childhood experiences.

Commentary: In answering this question there should be no problem in finding suitable material. But the secret of success here is your ability to show *the extent to which* these films or programmes are made to appeal to people of all ages.

Of course, the term 'the extent to which' means that you can say it does or it doesn't or it does, but not entirely.

17. Flashback (or analepsis) is a common technique used by film and TV programme makers.

Commentary: It can be used to explain events and give the audience information about characters prior to the beginning of the film. It can also be used to give information about events and characters that take place elsewhere during the same timescale of the film – though sometimes this can be achieved by split-screen technology.

Sometimes, with TV programmes, it takes place before the beginning of the programme narrative to remind viewers of what happened the previous week.

18. Life is made up of missed opportunities, someone once claimed.

Commentary: Certainly film and TV programme makers base much material on the concept. A film such as *Sliding Doors* makes clear the effect that missed opportunities can have. But even soaps can make use of missed opportunities in their characters' lives.

19. Questions about one particular scene are frequently asked in drama and fiction, and here it is in the film and TV drama section.

Commentary: The expression 'techniques used in the scene' gives you the chance to discuss all kinds of aspects of a scene from a film. Film and TV technology – wide-screen, colour, split-screen, sound, 3-D effects – all can help to make a scene memorable, as can the camera person's skill and the quality of acting.

Choose a scene from a film you know well and make sure that you can deal with the instruction to 'show *how* the techniques used in the scene gave you fresh insight into aspects of the text as a whole'. In other words, it isn't enough to deal with the scene; to achieve a good grade it is essential to show how the scene contributed not only to your better understanding of the text as a whole, but how it gave you fresh insight into the text. Did it make you re-assess the text or make you see it in a different light?

PRACTICE PAPER G   CLOSE READING WORKED ANSWERS

PASSAGE 1

1. (*a*) There is only one answer, though be vigilant because there are two parts to it. The answer can be found by a careful reading of the text (U).

> **TOP EXAM TIP**
>
> Remember: you **must** use your own words when a question is coded **U**.

Answer: Although Stephen Hawking is physically immobile (1), nevertheless he knows that his mind is totally free (1).

Commentary: Be careful to ensure that you read all that is connected to the question – in this case it is because he is so *physically* immobile that he is so aware of how free his mind is. Unless you mention the physical immobility (i.e. give the marker a gloss on the expression 'I cannot move and I have to speak through a computer'), then you cannot get full marks.

(*b*) Questions such as this (U) are useful because they help you to recognise the ways in which the points made by the author are developed.

Answer: Hawking realises that he is able to find out (a) if time travel is achievable (1); (b) if we can find a route to travel back to the past and forward to the future (1); and (c) if it is possible to employ the laws of nature as we know them to develop and conquer time travel (1).

Commentary: You already know how important it is to use your own words when answering (U) questions, but sometimes there is no alternative to the words used by the writer. In this case, it would be somewhat ridiculous to try to transform 'time travel' and 'laws of nature' into your own words.

> **HINT** It's a good idea to number or bullet point the questions to make your answer as clear as possible.

(*c*) You need to be aware of the functions of words in a sentence (A).

Answer: 'ultimately' (1).

Commentary: The adverb 'ultimately' can mean 'in the end', 'eventually', 'in the final instance', but it can also mean 'highest' (as in 'ultimate authority') or 'that which cannot be surpassed', which is the way it is used here. The word 'ultimately' is modifying the verb 'use', making clear that to ask if human beings can use the laws of nature to become masters of time travel is the highest or most important of the three questions asked.

2. The answer to this code U question is again in the text, in lines 6 and 7.

Answer: Physicists pay attention to the fourth dimension (1) – that is, in addition to length, breadth, and height, physicists regard time as another kind of measurement – measurement in time (1).

Commentary: It's really just a question of extracting the answer from lines 6–14.

> **HINT** There are 2 marks, therefore make two points.

3. Now we have to look at the writer's use of analogy to show *how* the language used conveys the idea of science fiction. Code A question – language analysis.

Answer: Word choice: the words 'time traveller' suggest the idea of a person travelling through time, an idea we associate with science fiction (1); also the phrase 'a brave, perhaps foolhardy individual' helps to convey the idea of science fiction because this phrase is one we would associate with characterisation – an aspect of fiction (1).

Sentence structure: the sentence in lines 17–19 is climactic in structure, building up to the main point at the end of the sentence 'emerges who knows when', a phrase that suggests both mystery (we don't know what will happen) and time (we don't know the point in time when the traveller will emerge at the end of his time travel) – all ideas associated with science fiction (2).

Commentary: Before you begin to answer a language question, think of all aspects of language – word choice, sentence structure, tone, imagery, punctuation. You could score all 3 marks for this question by using word choice alone. We could have used 'time travel movies', where the word 'movie' certainly suggests fiction and 'time travel' suggests science fiction. Mostly the answer comes from the fourth sentence, using word choice and sentence structure. What is remarkable is Hawking's use of climax with this sentence – he creates the build-up by inserting phrases – 'a brave', 'perhaps foolhardy individual', 'prepared for who knows what' and 'steps into the time tunnel', all of which are piled up before the climactic point 'and emerges who knows when'. The main thing is to link the points you make to the task – conveying the idea of science fiction. The answer above makes four points.

> **HINT** With language questions, always make sure you link the points you make to the task specified in the question.

4. A code A/U question, this time requiring a careful reading of the lines, but also a recognition of the technique of analogy.

Answer: He makes the idea easier to understand by using the analogy of the science fiction film (1), which portrays a machine that uses up a great deal of power (1) in order to tunnel a way through time (1) thus allowing the intrepid time traveller to travel along the tunnel and emerge in another time (1). Any three of the above points for 3 marks.

Commentary: You must be able to recognise the device of analogy – in this case the sci-fi time travel film. The writer goes on to demonstrate how this enormous machine uses up vast quantities of energy to fashion a tunnel in time, thus allowing the time traveller a route through time so that he can enter the tunnel and then emerge in a different period in time. The answer requires recognition of the analogy and then an explanation of how the analogy helps the reader understand the concept of time travel.

5. (a) There are 3 marks, therefore make sure that you make three points (U).

Answer: The tunnel or wormhole has within it a powerful vacuum-like force (1) which sucks in space and time allowing them to materialise (1) again in another universe (1).

Commentary: Negative energy is the opposite of energy, therefore it must be like a vacuum, and since it is 'pulling space and time' into the tunnel, it must be a very powerful vacuum; once space and time have been consumed by the tunnel, they emerge into a different universe. You need to condense these ideas into three main points.

> **HINT** Where you are asked to give the meaning of an expression, check the number of marks available and then look carefully at the expression to see which points you have to deal with – in this case 'negative energy', 'pulls space and time into the mouth of the tunnel' and 'emerging in another universe'.

(b) 1 mark for each of the stages of the argument (U).

Answer:
   i. Nothing is perfectly smooth or flat – everything is covered in holes or wrinkles (1);
   ii. it's easy to prove this fact in the dimensions of length, breadth and height (1);
  iii. but such wrinkles or holes also exist in time (1);
   iv. as we go smaller and smaller, we eventually reach a place called quantum foam (1);
   v. it's here that wormholes exist, linking separate places and different times (1).

Commentary: You are asked about the stages in an argument or line of thought, which means you ignore anything that is merely opinion.

> **HINT** Throughout your Higher course, it can be valuable (a) to note the difference in various texts between facts and opinions; and (b) to note the ways in which writers use language to express fact and to express opinion.

6. (*a*) Since all two-part questions are linked, make sure you read both parts before answering the first question.

Answer: The tone is fairly obviously humorous (1).

Commentary: Questions about tone are not as difficult as many candidates think – in this case, it's quite easy. There is something amusing about the idea of the dinosaurs 'witnessing' the landing of the spaceship, but here you aren't asked to justify the tone, only identify it.

(*b*) Just use your common sense (U).

Answer: Since the dinosaurs roamed the earth a very long time ago (1), the sentence illustrates the fact that time travel could go back millions of years (1).

Commentary: Dinosaurs clearly roamed the earth in the past (65 million years ago) and since the writer suggests that they may witness a space ship landing, the sentence is illustrating the idea that time travellers could go back millions of years in time.

7. You just need to read the text carefully (U), though you have to pay attention to the word 'exactly'. It's not enough just to say 'paradox gives them nightmares' – you need to explain the nature of the paradox for 2 marks. Use your own words!

Answer: The nature of the paradox, i.e. the idea that a traveller going back in time could shoot himself or even get killed (1), gives them nightmares (1) because such a man could not then return to the present (1).

Commentary: What disturbs cosmologists is the fact that travel back in time leaves it open for the time traveller to disturb or alter the past, so that when the traveller returns to the present, everything has changed. The example is the man who goes back in time and shoots his former self or his grandfather before the latter helped to conceive his father. How could he then exist in the present? It's the stuff of nightmares, especially for those people, such as cosmologists, concerned with time travel.

8. Make sure you use your own words (code U questions require your own words) – it's the idea that you have to get the gist of.

Answer: In this case, the writer means that for Person A to kill off the source of his existence (1) such that Person A could never have existed (1) breaks a fundamental law of the universe (1).

Commentary: Since the universe works on the principle of cause and effect (a billiard ball cannot move unless something moves it), the effect of any cause cannot be impossibility (a billiard ball cannot simply stop being a billiard ball without cause). Similarly, a man cannot simply not exist without a sufficient cause and to have one's grandfather killed before one's father is born would make it impossible for oneself to exist and that cannot happen within the laws of cause and effect.

9. Conclusion questions crop up from time to time. Just think about the purpose of conclusions. Such questions require analysis (A) and evaluation (E). And remember, you can argue that it isn't effective or that it is in some ways but not in others.

Answer: In this case, the final sentence captures in one image the two aspects of the passage – it picks up on the earlier remark about dinosaurs, creating a rounding-off effect (1), but more importantly it underlines the fact that history cannot be altered – a main point of the passage (1).

Commentary: There are only 2 marks available, therefore you only need to make 2 points. What is noticeable about the sentence is the rhythm, created by the repetition of the A (a dissapointment) for B (a relief) structure; as well as the use of contrast – what is a disappointment for one is a relief for the other. There is also the use of alliteration in 'disappointment for dinosaur hunters' and the subtle alliteration of hunters and historians. All of these devices go a long way to making the sentence memorable and therefore a good conclusion. The sentence also reiterates the idea about dinosaurs and underlines the idea that history cannot be altered.

PASSAGE 2

10. (*a*) The answer to this question (coded U) is an important part of the overall argument of the passage.

Answer: They are reasonably sure that the machine could provide the right environment (1) to make time travel possible (1).

Commentary: The answer is contained in the first sentence, although, since the second sentence develops the idea, reference to it would be perfectly acceptable. Just make sure that you use your own words.

(b) Be careful in answering this U question: you were told to read from line 1 to line 11 – and you need to read the whole of the second paragraph to find the answer.

Answer: Scientists do not accept the Russians' beliefs because the LHC was not designed to permit time travel (1) but to explore currently unknown activities among particles smaller than atoms (1).

Commentary: The difficulty is in dealing with the term 'subatomic particles', but as long as you get the gist of the meaning, then that is acceptable. Note that you are asked *why* the other scientists don't believe the Russians, therefore you have to give reasons and not just repeat the fact (as the first sentence of the paragraph does) that scientists don't believe the LHC will produce conditions conducive to time travel.

> **HINT** When you are told to read a certain number of lines, make sure that you read them all – carefully.

11. Another code U. You need to know what is meant by 'on what basis', an expression similar in meaning to 'what are the grounds for': both are asking you to give the reasons for something – in this case you are being asked for the reasons upon which Cox bases his claim.

Answer: Cox bases his claim on the fact that the speed of time passing on the ground is at a rate different from (1) the speed at which it travels in a satellite circling the earth (1).

Commentary: You have to get the gist of the fifth paragraph, however surprising its content may be.

> **HINT** Get to know what phrases such as 'on what basis' are asking you to do.

12. (a) A two part type question (a) and (b) – read both parts before you answer (a).

   Part (a) is a code U question – use your own words.

Answer: It was another attempt to write a novel based on time travel that revived interest in the subject.

Commentary: One simple point for 1 mark – make sure you use your own words *as far as possible*.

(b) The answer (U) requires a careful reading of the lines and an explanation of what, according to the writer, gave rise to the theory of wormholes.

Answer: The theory of 'wormholes' was the brainchild of a cosmologist, Kip Thorne (1), in response to a request by the novelist, Carl Sagan, to create a possible method by which travellers could get from one end of the universe to another without having to exceed the speed of light (1).

Commentary: Note that you are not asked to explain the theory – only how it arose. The answer really begins in line 36 with the paragraph starting 'When Carl Sagan, the American astronomer, was writing his 1986 novel' – he contacted his cosmologist friend, Kip Thorne, to ask him to explain a way by which a time traveller could travel a vast distance in space without having to travel faster than the speed of light. Thorne came up with the idea that by manipulating black holes it might be possible to invent a wormhole through space-time such that a traveller could go from one part of the universe to another in seconds. The idea was subsequently developed. You need to select the two most salient points from the above.

13. Again check page 6 to ensure you know all about what constitutes a good conclusion. Here it is worth 3 marks, therefore you need to make three points. You have to analyse the language (A) in order to evaluate the effectiveness (E).

Answer: The fact that it is a single sentence paragraph (1), therefore isolated (1) and thereby made dramatic (1), makes it an effective conclusion.

Commentary: You could also say that the repetition of 'crazy' draws attention to it, highlighting the idea that time travel is crazy but the 'just a bit' modifies the sense of it being crazy, suggesting that the idea isn't entirely crazy.

Also, beginning with 'So' is unusual, though here it has the feel of a conclusion since we often begin the conclusive part of an argument with 'so'.

Finally, the sentence is also a minor sentence – i.e. it is verbless, further drawing attention to its meaning, that time travel is crazy but not too crazy. Any of these for 1 mark each.

BOTH PASSAGES

14. The subject of time travel won't necessarily appeal to everyone, but this question allows you to state which of the two passages managed to hold your interest in the subject. But, of course, you must make reference to BOTH passages in your answer. The question, then, is very clearly (and not altogether surprisingly) asking you to deal with the ideas of both passages: which is the more effective in sustaining your interest in the possibility of time travel.

Commentary: What matters isn't the length of your answer but its quality. Avoid simply making a list of straightforward points, but ensure that your answer is (a) grammatically accurate, (b) formal in tone, (c) convincing in its presentation of your understanding of *both* passages, and (d) includes some credible evaluative comment.

Although you must deal with both passages, you should concentrate on the passage that presents for you the more interesting arguments about the possibility of time travel. Make sure that you include thoughtful, evaluative comment – make clear why you think your choice presents the more interesting line of thought.

See question 11 on page 72 for a guide to the marking criteria.

> **HINT** Your answer should be in the form of a mini-essay – make sure that you write grammatically and that your tone is formal.

PRACTICE PAPER G   CRITICAL ESSAY WORKED ANSWERS

Section A – Drama

1. This is a question about character.

> **HINT** It is very often how you deal with the second set of instructions that determines the mark you receive.

Commentary: Note that, as is mostly the case, you are asked to do TWO things: (1) explain how the main character's internal conflict is presented by the dramatist and then (2) show how that conflict is used to shape the final scenes of the play.

It is really important that you spend plenty of time, *BEFORE* you sit the exam, thinking about the conflict that is presented in the play you are studying. You could say that the definition of drama is conflict – you can certainly say that you cannot have drama without conflict. In the kind of plays you are studying there will be *internal* conflict as well as external. The protagonist will be in conflict with individuals around him or with society in general, but also he or she will suffer conflict within him or herself. Hamlet, Macbeth, Othello, King Lear, John Proctor, Willie Loman, Joe Keller, and Eddie Carbone all suffer internal conflict.

But the important question to ask yourself is: *how* does this internal conflict determine the outcome of the drama? How does the internal conflict shape the outcome of the play? The important word is 'shape'. What the question is really

> **TOP EXAM TIP**
>
> With all plays, it is important first of all that you think through the themes of the play – and by that I mean the themes that *you* detect. As long as you can find evidence from the text that supports your chosen theme, then that's what counts.

asking is how do the ways in which the protagonist handles the internal conflict affect the outcome? For example, what internal conflict does John Proctor suffer? His previous relationship with Abigail versus his strong sense of morality and genuine love for his wife? And how does that conflict shape or contribute to what happens? Does it affect, for example, his change of heart, his sudden decision to face the scaffold after all? What internal conflict does Willie Loman suffer and how do the ways in which he handles it affect his decision to commit suicide?

Think very seriously about the nature of conflict in the play you are studying.

2. This is a question about hatred and motives.

> **HINT** ⟩ Think about hatred in its widest sense.

Commentary: Do any of the characters in the play(s) you are studying feel hatred for another character? Or for society in general? Does that hatred form a motive for their behaviour? Think of Iago: his hatred for Othello is obvious and, indeed, he makes it clear in his soliloquies how much he hates the Moor. What about Claudius – does he hate Hamlet? Does Eddie Carbone hate Rodolpho?

Who is the villain in the play you are studying? And does he or she feel hatred? Does hatred form a powerful motivating force?

3. Questions about setting appear fairly frequently – and this one asks about how setting reflects the wider concerns of the drama.

> **HINT** ⟩ Think about *time* as well as place when you consider setting. Too many candidates forget that time is part of setting, along with weather and atmosphere.

Commentary: Again, think about the play you are studying. Whatever it is, setting will be an important technique used by the dramatist to help portray the theme or an aspect of character. Remember that this question is asking how setting is used by the dramatist *to reflect the wider issues of the play*. Take *The Crucible*: first of all, what are the wider issues of that play? Ostensibly, it's about witchcraft and the need that the Salem community feels to stamp it out. But then matters get complicated when others use the feelings about witchcraft as an opportunity to settle old scores. Witchcraft is really a metaphor: the witchcraft at Salem can be compared with the hunt for communists in mid 20th century USA or, indeed, any other irrational pursuit of attitudes thought to be inimical to society's wellbeing.

Next you have to ask yourself: how important is Salem, the place, its politics, its atmosphere, its society to the issues of witchcraft and then to these wider issues of the play? By setting the play in Salem, Miller can exploit to the full the characters and attitudes that led to the witch-hunt.

Then what about *Othello*? How does the sophisticated society of Venice reflect the issues at the beginning of the play, how does the storm reflect and/or suggest the storm to come, in what ways is the setting of Cyprus important in bringing about the tragedy that happens?

In all drama, the setting can play a vital part in the portrayal of the themes. It is often a kind of metaphor for the wider issues – and don't forget the pathetic fallacy: the ways in which weather can represent issues and even character downfall.

4. This is a straightforward question – you are given a choice of themes and either your play reflects/portrays one of those themes or it doesn't.

> **TOP EXAM TIP**
>
> Make sure you interpret the terms of the question in the widest possible sense.

Commentary: Make sure that you interpret terms in their widest sense – love, for example, is a hugely important theme in *Romeo and Juliet*: obviously the love between Romeo and Juliet, but there is parental love, the love friends have for each other, and there is also a kind of analysis of what 'love' means – is it sex (the scene at the beginning where love is regarded in the crudest terms of sexual aggression towards women), or is it love-making (Romeo in the beginning is upset because Rosaline won't let him have sexual intercourse) or is it something almost religious and dignified (the scene when Romeo and Juliet first meet)?

SECTION B – PROSE

Prose fiction

5. Clearly you need to know what 'unrequited love' means, but if your novel deals with it, the chances are high that the term has been mentioned in class. (Love which is unreturned by one of the partners – loving someone who doesn't love you back.)

Commentary: Not all novels will have unrequited love as their theme, but it is there in *The Great Gatsby*: though Gatsby sees Daisy as the object of his desire and his love, she doesn't quite reciprocate. But the important question is: how does the nature of this relationship reflect the wider concerns of the text – and there you need to explore the metaphorical aspects of character. If Gatsby comes to represent America and Daisy his dream, we can see how or in what ways the unrequited love suggests that America will never attain its dream.

Does the novel you are studying in any way present such a relationship – unrequited love – and, if so, in what ways is that unrequited love representative of aspects of the novel's themes?

 Be prepared to see character (as well as setting) as metaphorical.

6. Quite often, in fiction, our sympathy or affection or even feelings for the main character do not emerge until later in the text. This question is directed at that kind of novel.

 Quite often, what happens to the main character forms for him or her a learning experience – he or she changes as a result of experience and it is at the point of change that our sympathies are engaged.

Commentary: In *The Power and the Glory* by Graham Greene, for example, it usually takes a reader some time to feel affection for the Whisky Priest, a man who has shown moral weakness, an alcoholic who has fathered a child, a man who, in his younger days, was smug and self-satisfied but who now, chased by the Lieutenant, feels guilt for his sins, and who develops kindness and a sense of morality and dignity. He is quite unlikeable, almost despicable, to begin with but he gains the reader's respect and even affection as the novel develops.

 In Greene's *The Power and the Glory*, the characters of the Whisky Priest and the Lieutenant remain nameless, the effect of which is to draw attention to their metaphorical significance.

7. This is the short story question. Isolation is often a theme in short stories and it can be explored in a number of ways, thus making comparison fairly straightforward.

Commentary: As with all Critical Essay questions, make sure you widen the question in your answer. Isolation can apply to individuals isolated from their community, but also from their family, or to those who feel isolated within a marriage or relationship.

 Make sure that you don't interpret terms in a narrow way.

Isolation can also be physical – in *Uneasy Homecoming*, Connie is isolated from all the other houses because hers is the only house at the other side of the bay – such isolation makes it easy for the burglar. But isolation can also be a feeling of exclusion, as in *Flowers* by Robin Jenkins, where Margaret feels isolated from the other children because she has been evacuated to a rural community, far away from her urban background.

Isolation can also be within a marriage – Mary Maloney in *Lamb to the Slaughter* by Roald Dahl feels isolated within her marriage, especially after the conversation with her husband before dinner, and the father feels very isolated from his teenage son in *Father and Son* by Bernard MacLaverty.

You should also consider reading *Short Cuts* by Raymond Carver – a collection of short stories set in America. Many of his main characters suffer greatly from isolation.

8. Main characters invariably learn something about themselves or about human nature from the experiences they undergo in the course of the novel, and disillusionment is one aspect of the human condition that many protagonists experience.

Commentary: Isserley, the main character in *Under the Skin* by Michel Faber, is one such character who becomes significantly disillusioned as the novel progresses. Though technically not 'human', she grows increasingly disillusioned with her job, her colleagues, and the way she has to live her life.

In *The Cone Gatherers* by Robin Jenkins, there are a number of characters who become disillusioned with their lot – Duror, perhaps, being the main one. But to a certain extent you could argue that Neil becomes disillusioned with those around him.

Prose Non-fiction

9. All writers, especially of short works, do tend to pay a great deal of attention to detail.

> **HINT**   Prose non-fiction (essays and journalism) tends to be restricted to George Orwell – *A Hanging*, *Marrakech*, *Shooting an Elephant* – though you should remember that there are a number of worthy columnists writing in today's papers (some of whose work appears in this book as passages for Close Reading).

Commentary: But the question is about how the writer *creates* and *uses* detail to contribute to the impact that the text has on the reader. Look at the beginning of *Marrakech* by Orwell:

> When you walk through a town like this – two hundred thousand inhabitants, of whom at least twenty thousand own literally nothing except the rags they stand up in – when you see how the people live, and still more easily they die, it is always difficult to believe that you are walking among human beings.

He tells the reader the number of inhabitants – 'two hundred thousand' – a detail that gives the piece authenticity and makes the reader feel as though he/she is there with him. That he tells us that 'at least twenty thousand own literally nothing except the rags they stand up in' is a detail that convinces the reader that Orwell is not only in charge of his subject matter but that he was actually present to find out these details. Not only do you see how they live, but you also see *how easily they die*. This is further detail that convinces the reader of what Orwell actually witnessed and his grasp of the situation. He uses the detail, then, to convince and to establish authenticity.

You could also mention how he uses sentence structure to highlight the detail, but that's for you to work out for yourself.

10. Many, many travel books deal with journeys; it depends what you have studied. But be warned – the question is about structure, therefore you really do need to have studied the book.

Commentary: You should consider such structural features as the exposition (how the book is introduced); what and how it deals with its subject matter – country by country, town by town, journey by journey or a mixture of these three or any other possibilities; the way in which it is narrated; the tone of the language used. You should also think about the ways in which the text is developed by the writer; his or her use of illustrative and/or entertaining anecdote; the use of photographs; and how it is concluded.

> **HINT**   The problem with biography, autobiography and travel writing is that it is too easy to be seduced into talking about subject matter rather than answering the question asked.

11. A somewhat cruel question, perhaps, in that it restricts you to material written this century, which instantly rules out Orwell, many of whose essays would be ideal for this question, especially *Marrakech*. But you see the importance of reading the question carefully!

> **HINT** — There are some excellent writers/newspaper columnists whose material is well written and highly relevant to the 21st century – writers such as Ian Bell, Melanie Reid, Ruth Wishart and many others from papers such as *The Herald*, *The Sunday Herald*, *The Scotsman*, *The Guardian*, *The Independent*, *The Observer*.

Commentary: The task set is about how the author uses language to create impact. Now you know what 'language' involves from your Close Reading: word choice, sentence structure, imagery, tone, punctuation. Since such questions are not unusual, though they may be asked in a different form, it is worth knowing how the writer of the non-fiction you are studying uses all these aspects of language to create effect or to shape meaning.

Section C – Poetry

12. This is the particular/universal question in one of its many disguises.

Commentary: The question asks you to examine the particular story or incident or situation and then to examine its universal application: it is seeing literature as metaphor. Whatever poem you are studying, of course it is about itself, but it is also about something greater than itself. The poem will have wider implications, more universal concerns, many of which only emerge after several readings. For example, *Little Red Riding Hood* is a tale about a little girl who is so deceived by a bad wolf, disguised as her grandmother, that she nearly ends up being eaten by him – you know the story.

But this tale also has metaphorical significance – the very fact that the colour *Red* is in the title suggests danger. It can be regarded as a tale about the dangers of a forest, the vulnerability of little girls, the ability of some people to appear genuine and caring while all the while they are prepared ready to destroy you. It is a tale about innocence and predatory wickedness.

Many, if not most, poems are capable of being interpreted in that way – they are significant in themselves but they also have universal application, and it can take time to recognise fully what the universal applications are. Think of the poems you have studied in that way – what do they say about the particular situation or incident and then what comments does the particular make about the wider aspect of the human condition? Some of Edwin Muir's poems and Ted Hughes's poems would be ideal for this question.

13. Interpret 'communication' in its widest possible sense: language of any kind, including singing, dancing, spoken and written language.

> **HINT** — The poetry section is often quite narrow in its range of choices. You can find that the poems you have studied cannot form the answer to any of the questions!

Commentary: Not that many poems may 'fit' a question about communication, but some will. Those of you who have studied any of the Romantic poets – Wordsworth, Coleridge, Keats, Byron, Shelley – and even some war poets, such as Owen, will find poetry that deals with communication.

14. There will always be one question that asks for a comparison between two poems.

> **HINT** — Do not, under any circumstances, tackle this question if you have not been prepared for it in class.

Commentary: Not that many poems deal with the subject matter of hope, though some will imply a hopeful outlook; to find two such poems will not be easy, but that's a measure of the poetry section. Some of Shakespeare's sonnets express hope, though often in a surprising or ironic way. Robert Frost, too, suggests hope in some of his poetry.

> **HINT** — When comparing poems (or anything else for that matter), make sure that you do it point by point and don't deal with one poem and then the other. There have to be points of comparison and/or contrast.

15. On the other hand, many poems explore the ideas of loneliness or separation.

HINT > Learn to spell both 'loneliness' and 'separation' correctly!

Commentary: In this task you are asked to examine the techniques. Make sure, with every poem you study, that you are aware of the concerns or themes of the poem and the techniques by which those themes are portrayed.

And remember that there are language techniques as well as poetic techniques.

Section D – Film and TV Drama

16. Several soap operas deal with difficult subjects.

Commentary: In answering this question you would have to make clear what you mean by a 'difficult subject'. You would also need to say in what way(s) you find it is being sensitively – or insensitively – handled. The question does say 'to what extent', therefore you can say that it isn't being sensitively handled or that the way the subject is being handled is partially sensitive.

If you think along these lines, you will find the way into the question easy – you first of all define what you mean by difficult subject, then say how the film or programme makers established that subject, then show the extent to which you feel that it has been handled sensitively.

17. Many films use flashback (also known as analepsis).

Commentary: Note, for example, the flashback used in *The Lord of the Rings* trilogy. Others use split-screen technology, which is a visual way of showing two or more images on the one screen: the BBC drama, *Spooks*, for example, uses split-screen narration to indicate simultaneous action in different locations. Some use a combination of colour and monochrome and others use slow and fast motion.

But remember that the task is to show *how* the film or programme makers use these methods to enhance the ways in which the story is told. Print narrative, by definition, has to be linear, but film and TV technology can allow for non-linear narration. Or can it?

18. Be carefull: this question asks you to do quite a lot.

Commentary: You really need to follow a three part structure: (a) say how the film or programme makers portray the main character; (b) show the nature of the conflict; and (c) go on to say how the situation (conflict) is resolved. Now you don't have to deal with everything in this (a), (b), (c) structure, but you do really have to show the ways in which the main character is shown to be in conflict with his or her society (or community or social group).

HINT > In Section D, if your answer is based on the film of a book, make sure you deal exclusively with film and the filmic techniques.

19. There are a number of TV dramas that deal with friendship.

Commentary: In answering this question, very discerning candidates will note that the question involves the 'nature' of friendship and the task specifies that you have to examine how character and circumstance are used to reveal the 'various aspects of friendship'.

Again, remember you are dealing with film and TV drama techniques and not with the techniques of fiction.

PRACTICE PAPER H   CLOSE READING WORKED ANSWERS

PASSAGE 1

1. (*a*) The question demands (as do all code U questions) your own words – the answer lies in the text.

> **TOP EXAM TIP**
>
> Remember: you **must** use your own words when a question is coded **U**.

Answer: It seems that the UK government recognises that any steps forward in cutting greenhouse gases are illusory (a misapprehension) (1) while the Scottish government seem to be advocating that what is needed is actual achievement (1).

Commentary: The answer is contained in the one-sentence paragraph. The UK government has a chief environmental scientist who claims that progress on such cuts is an illusion whereas the Scottish government's potential policies would suggest that they have had enough of illusion and now want action – two points, therefore 2 marks but they have to be in your own words. The word 'illusion' is difficult to put into your own words – 'illusory' would be acceptable, though it's maybe better to use a word such as delusion or misapprehension.

(*b*) This is a language question and therefore code A.

Answer: The policy document sees the car at the very centre of the plan for curbing greenhouse gas emissions because it is largely to blame (1) ('contributing culprit') for causing us to miss the set objectives in reducing damage to the surroundings and atmosphere (1).

Commentary: It puts it 'centre-stage' as 'one of the contributing culprits' to the 'current failure to meet environmental targets'. Now, you haven't to put that into your own words – you have to comment on the language used. 2 marks means that you have to make two points or one point developed.

2. (*a*) Be careful. In Standard Grade, when asked to provide evidence, you are allowed to quote from the passage, but this is a U-coded question, meaning that you have to use your own words.

Answer: The evidence is listed: we agree to official target contracts at major world conferences (1), we agree to deadlines for meeting those contracts (1), and we even say we'll guarantee certain outcomes and then promise to do more (1).

Commentary: Read lines 9–11 very carefully. Here, there are three sentences listing all the things Britain agrees to and then, in the fourth sentence, it is made clear that we don't reach the targets we claim to meet. The evidence is listed in the three sentences, each worth 1 mark. The skill is in putting it all into your own words.

(*b*) A language question and therefore code A because analysis is required.

Answer: The declamatory repetition of 'We sign up', 'We agree to', and 'We have also announced' creates a climactic build up (1) which emphasises the extent and range of all that we promise (1). This use of anaphora then helps to sharpen and draw attention to his argument which culminates in the sentence that makes clear that we meet none of these targets (1). Any two points for 2 marks.

Commentary: As well as the above points, mention could be made of the use of 'But' in the penultimate sentence, introducing a contrast and the 'And' in the final sentence, drawing attention to his argument that Scotland plans to do more.

3. (*a*) Another code A language question – and that means thinking about sentence structure, word choice, tone, imagery, punctuation.

> *HINT* Don't shy away from answering language questions using sentence structure. Quite often the question is most easily answered by an analysis of the structure of sentences – as is the case here.

Answer: The sentence beginning 'A lowering of speed limits' is in the form of an asyndetic list (1), each item of which builds up to the climactic 'big stick measures' (1) which is a clarification of what the writer means by life becoming more difficult for car users (1). The list itself reveals the range and extent of the measures involved (1).

> **HINT**
>
> Asyndetic lists (asyndeton) are lists which do not have conjunctions as part of their structure – the effect of which is often to indicate the range and extent of the items in the list or to create climax.
>
> Polysyndetic lists (polysyndeton) are lists which have conjunctions between each item in the list, the effect of which is to create a regular rhythm and the impression that the items are causally linked and/or that each item carries equal weight. The overall effect is to draw attention to the list and its climactic structure.

Commentary: You can hardly fail to notice that the sentence beginning 'A lowering of speed limits ...' is in the form of an asyndetic list – the effect of which is to create a build-up to the climactic 'big stick measures designed to change behaviour'. Each of the items illustrates the statement 'making life difficult and more expensive for car users', thus clarifying the writer's meaning. Furthermore, the climax – 'big stick measures' – is a clarification of what is meant by life becoming more difficult and more expensive since that is how behaviour will be changed.

(b)   This language question (A) is restricted to imagery, which usually means there's a simile or metaphor that you have to analyse. You are also restricted to lines 18–23, the second part of the same paragraph. The instruction is to refer to more than one example, which means that if you choose to analyse two examples, your answer needs to be developed. You could, of course, analyse four examples in a less developed way.

> **HINT**
>
> Remember that when analysing a metaphor you should refer to the literal meaning as well as the figurative meaning.

Answer: First of all, the writer mentions that Holyrood has a 'raft' of ideas for genuine encouragement to motorists – a 'raft' is something man-made and enables people and objects to stay afloat safely and it has come to be used to mean a very large amount (1). In this context, it means that there are many ideas 'floating around' to be used as means of encouragement (1). Also, the idea of a carrot being used as an incentive is a metaphorical use of the physical carrot fed to a donkey in order to encourage it to move (1). Here the image of the 'carrot' makes clear that there are a number of incentives to encourage drivers/car users to accept the measures (1).

Commentary: You can see that the paragraph is divided into two parts – the first part deals with the 'big stick measures' aimed at car users whereas the second part deals with 'the measures of encouragement' – and it is here, line 18 onwards, that you are asked about imagery and *how* its use helps to convey the encouragement. You should note right away that there are several images – the writer talks about the 'raft of ideas' and 'carrots alongside the stick'; he also talks of Holyrood wanting to 'explore all avenues' within the 'bigger environmental picture'. But you really need only select two examples of imagery for analysis for 2 marks each.

4. (a)   You have to put the expression into your own words – therefore code U.

Answer: The expression refers to a voting public (1) who are bored by (1) or are against (1) the idea of cutting greenhouse gases.

> **HINT**
>
> 3 marks suggests that there are three words that you have to account for.

Commentary: The expression 'an apathetic, or worse antagonistic, electorate' has three terms, the meanings of which you must make clear – 'apathetic', 'antagonistic' and 'electorate'.

(b)   Another U-coded question, the answer to which is clearly in the text.

Answer: The smoking ban succeeded because an informed public recognised the health advantages of (1), and therefore the necessity for (1), banning smoking in public places.

Commentary: The answer lies in the following sentence: 'The smoking ban pioneered by Holyrood succeeded because the public had already accepted the need for change and were clear about the benefits'. Put this into your own words.

(*c*) The term 'this ambiguity' refers to the ambiguity he has already mentioned in the previous sentence. Because the question is really about the meaning of ideas/words, it is coded U.

Answer: The ambiguity is that while we may agree with some minor nods (1) in the direction of doing something about improving the environment (1) we'll protest strongly, even aggressively (1), against anything that causes considerable upset to our lives (1).

> **HINT** The demonstrative adjective 'this' takes an antecedent – i.e. a word or idea that goes before the use of the word 'this' and to which it refers.

Commentary: Ambiguity means that a word, phrase or sentence is capable of two meanings or interpretations – as is the case here.

5. Read carefully the beginning of the next paragraph for the answer to this code U question.

Answer: The green agenda has taken a back seat of late because (a) we are suffering severe cutbacks (1); (b) we are in a recession which means the economy is not expanding (1); and (c) unemployment is rising (1).

Commentary: The answer clearly lies in the second sentence – 'In the current austerity climate, where there is worry over the lack of growth and what this could mean in terms of job losses, the green agenda has suddenly taken a political back seat.' It has taken a back seat because of the current austerity climate, the lack of growth, job losses – three reasons, therefore 3 marks.

6. Another question restricting your analysis (A) to sentence structure. Be careful – although the mention of the lack of Scotland's integrated transport system is on lines 41–43, you are asked to analyse the sentence on lines 44–47.

> **HINT** Close Reading, you must remember, is a test of your reading skills, and if you misread the question there will be no forgiveness.

Answer: The sentences are structured as questions followed by one-word answers (1), the effect being to create a brevity and starkness which draw attention to the lack of an integrated transport system (1) and to the fact that the car is the centre of the problem (1). Any two points for 2 marks.

Commentary: Surprisingly, there are only 2 marks allocated to this question – and yet you could make many points. You can't help noticing that the sentences are in the form of questions and answers, and that the answers are one-word minor sentences, the effect of which is to draw attention to the lack of an integrated transport system.

7. Another U-coded question about meanings of ideas.

Answer: The unanswered question is how the government can bring about and direct (1) societal and political attitudes and behaviour (1) towards climate change.

Commentary: The answer to this question is made quite clear – it is 'how best to manage the cultural change which is the unavoidable logical end to their argument'. In other words (which is what you have to use!), the big unanswered question is how to bring about societal and political changes in people's attitudes and behaviour towards climate change.

PASSAGE 2

8. This question is coded A and is about sentence structure.

Answer: The first word of the sentence – 'These' – refers back to the radical plans mentioned in the previous sentence (1), and the sentence itself is in the form of a list (1) which conveys the extent and range of the plans mentioned (1).

Commentary: You can see immediately that the sentence is in the form of a list, but also that the sentence begins with the word 'These' – a demonstrative adjective, plural, which takes an antecedent. In this case the word 'These' is referring back to 'a further series of radical plans', which means that the whole sentence is an explanation of what the radical plans include. The list forms that explanation and the items in it convey the range and extent of the plans.

9. To answer this question (U) you need to work out how the words quoted are then developed in the following sentences.

Answer: The three terms are developed by further references to (a) the Scottish co-ordinator for the Association of British Drivers, who claimed that to introduce such curbs on cars would be 'political suicide' (1); (b) the CBI, who claimed that the £300 a year workplace levy would be another tax on businesses (1); and (c) the chief executive of the NFU in Scotland, who is against compulsory measures (1). Each point is worth 1 mark, giving 3 marks in all.

Commentary: He uses three terms – 'the ire of the car lobby', 'businesses' and 'farmers'. Next read on and see how each of these terms is developed: the car lobby anger is developed by the references to the Scottish co-ordinator for the Association of British Drivers who claimed that to introduce such curbs on cars would be 'political suicide'; the businesses reference is developed by mention of the CBI and their claim that the £300 a year workplace levy would be another tax on businesses; and the reference to farmers is developed by the quotation from the chief executive of the NFU in Scotland.

10. Be careful: the question isn't about the tone of what the doctor said but about the writer's attitude to what he said. It is coded A because analysis is required.

Answer: The writer chooses the word 'commended' (1), with its positive conotations, to suggest his approval of Dr Dixon's remarks (1).

Commentary: There is one word that clearly conveys the writer's attitude: the word 'commended' suggests the writer's approval of Dr Dixon's remarks.

11. You need to know the meanings of 'garnered', 'bouquets' and 'brickbats', but the context should help. Since the question is about meanings, it is coded U and requires your own words to be used.

Answer: It means that the proposals have gathered together lots of praise (1), and at the same time, much criticism (1).

Commentary: The expression 'that has already garnered' means that which has been already brought together, and since 'bouquets' suggests a bunch of flowers or a garland of flowers then, in its metaphorical sense, it must suggest praise or congratulations. On the other hand, 'brickbats' must suggest the opposite – abuse or criticism.

12. In this language question (A), you have to look for words that have positive connotations.

Answer: The positive side to the policies included in the report are reinforced by phrases such as 'boosting the membership' of car clubs, which means that there will be more car sharing (1) and 'offering grants' is a very positive incentive to get people to change their behaviour to protect the environment (1).

 HINT The connotation of a word means what the word suggests to you, the association that the word has for you.

Commentary: Here, there are many words suggesting the positive nature of the policies – 'boosting the membership' especially of car clubs suggests success at car sharing; 'free training' suggests that more drivers may take it up because it isn't going to cost them money; 'offering grants' is a positive incentive to get people to do what the government wants; 'plans for major investments in bus and rail facilities' suggests that more people will use public transport – a positive outcome; 'better travel planning' means that people will make use of more economical ways of getting about; 'incentives to shift freight from road to rail and water' suggests more carbon-friendly methods of transportation – any two of these for 1 mark each.

Both Passages

13. You have to choose which of the passages is the more thought-provoking about the Scottish Government's proposals for creating a low-carbon environment. Be careful though: however interested you are in the subject, you must **not** include your own ideas, but concentrate on the ideas of both passages.

Commentary: Note that you are being asked about ideas and not about style, therefore to reach top marks it must clearly and convincingly be about the writers' ideas. Also note that what matters isn't the length of your answer but its quality. Avoid simply making a list of straightforward points, but ensure that your answer is (a) grammatically accurate, (b) formal in tone, (c) convincing in its presentation of your understanding of *both* passages, and (d) includes some credible evaluative comment.

Although you must deal with both passages, you should concentrate on the passage that presents for you the more thought-provoking analysis of the Scottish Government's proposals. Include evaluative comment – make clear why you think your choice presents the more convincing argument.

See question 11 on page 72 for a guide to the marking criteria.

> **HINT** Because you have to make a choice about the passages, your answer isn't likely to treat both equally. But don't treat the second one scantily!

PRACTICE PAPER H   CRITICAL ESSAY WORKED ANSWERS

Section A – Drama

1. From time to time, the 'minor character' question appears either in the drama or the fiction section.

> **TOP EXAM TIP**
>
> Try to incorporate quotations into your own sentence structure, and certainly into your argument. Only if the quotation is long should you isolate it into a separate line.

Commentary: In *Hamlet*, for example, would you consider Horatio to be the minor character, or Ophelia? Look at the question – you have to consider his or her contribution to the outcome. Which character could you deal with most appropriately in answering that question? Claudius/Laertes/the Ghost all spring to mind. Then you should consider in what way(s) any of these characters contribute to the outcome – which is the death of so many characters at the end.

> **HINT** As part of your preparation for the exam, you should consider who you think is the minor character in the play and/or novel that you are reading. Then, you have to consider the importance of his or her role in the portrayal of the theme.

2. Stage techniques are usually made clear in the stage instructions – which means that when you study your text you should become familiar with the stage instructions.

Commentary: After the First World War (1914–18), many dramatists felt that the dramatic techniques of the 19th century – drawing room drama – were no longer able to express the concerns of a world still reeling from the horrendous experience of a war without precedence. The stage, many felt, had to be seen as something more than just a box with one wall missing and the audience had to be regarded as more than voyeurs. Williams, in plays such as *The Glass Menagerie*, introduced the idea of a narrator who is nevertheless a character in the play and can slip easily from one role to the other. He also introduced the idea of a screen onto which images relating to the story could be projected. Miller, especially in *Death of a Salesman*, used scenery in a representative way, and broke conventions of wall boundaries to indicate when the action was in the present and when it was in the past. Music, too, and lighting all began to play important representative roles in the production of what came to be known as *modernist* drama.

You must study your play at different levels and be aware of the stage instructions and all that they contribute to the overall effect of the drama.

3. This is the internal conflict question, but note that you have to deal with the ways in which the character is destroyed by the forces within him or her.

Commentary: You cannot have drama without conflict – it's the basis of all the drama, films, TV programmes that you know. In more straightforward drama the conflict is external – the goodies versus the baddies – but in the kind of drama you study (and most probably watch) conflict is also internal. One of the goodies suffers from conflict within him or herself. This question is asking you to think about that internal conflict and to determine the extent to which it brings about the downfall of the protagonist experiencing the conflict.

In some cases, the protagonist doesn't develop internal conflict until he or she learns from experience: Lady Macbeth, for example, doesn't really develop internal conflict until she realises that 'naught's had, all's spent', by which time the conflict within her is beginning to destroy her, leading to her suicide.

Macbeth, too, though reasonably untroubled at the beginning of the play, develops strong internal conflict by the end when he realises that he has gained very little by his actions.

When preparing your play, make sure that you understand the internal conflict suffered by the protagonist and how it leads to his or her downfall – it could be just one of the factors or it could be the major factor.

4. On the other hand, this question is asking you to deal with external conflict, about which you should know a great deal.

Commentary: You cannot really study a major drama text without working out the external conflict. In Shakespearean drama, it is usually fairly obvious: in *Romeo and Juliet*, it is love versus hate, the younger generation versus the older generation, and those are just two of the external conflicts; in *Othello*, it is loyalty versus betrayal, malice and dishonour versus love and honour; in *Macbeth*, it is duplicity and iniquity versus rectitude and goodness.

In more modern plays, perhaps the themes are not quite so grand: in *Death of a Salesman*, for example, the external conflict is between a man who is out of his time, a man whose values of loyalty and respect are at variance with the modern world and its cut-throat approach to business; it also deals with dreams and hopes and the ways in which they are at variance with reality. In *A Streetcar Named Desire*, the external conflict is between two characters who, in themselves, are representative of opposite sets of values – Blanche, the southern belle, with her delicacy and vulnerability, nevertheless representing a belief in family values, civilised behaviour and loyalty versus Stanley, the alpha male, caveman-like and brutal, representing the new America, industrialised and individual.

Section B – Prose

Prose fiction

5. Many novels deal with rural settings, but here you have to deal with it as a suitable backdrop for one or more of your chosen themes.

Commentary: Certainly *The Cone Gatherers* springs to mind, with its setting in the forest and the country estate. The woods, for example, can be seen variously as (a) the representation of paradise (and man's expulsion therefrom); (b) a representation of somewhere that merely witnesses human evil but doesn't prevent it; (c) a place that actually harbours evil; (d) a representation of Hell on earth.

The woods can also represent destruction and regeneration. Since they are to be cut down for the war effort and replanted, they can be seen as a symbol of regeneration. The cones for re-planting trees are normally imported, but because of the war they are being gathered locally (hence the reason for the cone gatherers). You can begin to see the symbolic representation of destruction and rebirth.

The point is that, however remote these woods are from the horrors of the war that is going on in the background (horrors of which the reader is constantly reminded, especially the killing of innocents and babies), nevertheless they do not provide any shelter from human degeneracy.

The setting also provides the background for the class struggle represented by Lady Runcie-Campbell and 'the lower orders', especially Neil and Calum. The struggle pervades the novel, and it is clearly articulated at the very beginning. Neil makes clear that he thinks there should be no difference between the classes. Neil mocks the fact that they live like monkeys – he says that, after all, they live in a box fit for monkeys.

There are several examples throughout the novel where Jenkins makes the relationship between the local setting and the wider world. In chapter one, for example, in the second paragraph, mention is made of a destroyer steaming seawards, aeroplanes flying over the wood, and the sound of gunshots – all symbols of war, all setting the local scene within the global context of war. Towards the end of the final chapter, as Lady Runcie-Campbell reaches the promontory, she sees 'a warship steam(ing) down the loch', a final reminder of the backdrop of war.

Another novel which exploits a rural (i.e. non-urban) setting is *Lord of the Flies*, where the paradisiacal island turns into a hellish inferno, brought about by the 'darkness of man's heart'.

6. This is a clear and straightforward invitation to deal with a humorous novel – and such things do exist! You are asked to show how the writer creates the humour and, then, go on to show how that humour contributes to the overall theme.

Commentary: The question cries out for, say, *Catch 22* by Joseph Heller or the even more accessible *Scotland Street* series by Alexander McCall Smith. The series begins with *44 Scotland Street* and the humour is created by McCall Smith's ability to create character, to create situation, and to exploit language in humorous ways. Your essay could be restricted to the presentation of the character of Bertie, a five-year-old, much put-upon boy, whose exploits are funny and hold almost an entire class of pretentious parents up to ridicule. This is satire of the very best order.

If you haven't already read any of this Scot's novels, it is perhaps time you made his acquaintance.

7. The short story question in this paper does not invite any comparison; instead you have to make clear that the stories you choose are interesting to read in themselves while making some universal comment.

Commentary: Iain Crichton Smith's *Telegram* would certainly be one such short story, the universality being hinted at by the fact that neither woman is actually named, though the fat woman is referred to as Sarah at one point. Somerset Maugham's *The Verger* would also fall into this category – we want to read on to find out what happens to Albert Edward Foreman after he leaves St Peter's, Neville Square, while at the same time recognising its more universal comments on how the less educated, especially those who can neither read nor write, are liable to be treated. The ending is superbly ironic.

8. Several novels spring immediately to mind because of their unusual narrative technique.

Commentary: Some American fiction can be quite experimental, such as *Fight Club* by Chuck Palahniuk, a novel narrated by a nameless character, a technique that becomes even more complicated as the novel develops.

Of course, Heller's *Catch 22* employs an unusual narrative technique, which to begin with is very confusing, though all becomes clear at the end – the confusing and illogical nature of war is portrayed by the confusing and illogical narrative style.

Even *The Heart of Darkness* by Joseph Conrad is unusual in that it is presented as a framed narrative (a story which is framed or embedded in another story): as the men wait in the boat on the Thames for the tide to turn, one of them relates Marlow's story to the others. The effect is to distance the narrative from Conrad himself – the story could be seen to be critical of the Belgian monarchy – but it also allows the story to be told as darkness falls on the River Thames, capturing and echoing the details of Marlow's narrative.

Prose Non-fiction

9. You are asked to analyse the ways in which a writer's technique captures and sustains a text concerning scientific or philosophical issues.

Commentary: This may not appeal to many people, but you could consider *A Short History of Nearly Everything*, a general science book by Bill Bryson. Its success is its straightforwardness and its humour.

10. A world that is different from your own can be taken in the geographical sense or the political/cultural sense.

Commentary: You are asked to deal with the way in which this world has been presented in the text, therefore you need to concentrate on the writer's style and language. Orwell's essays would make an ideal subject.

11. A text which tells of someone whose life story is totally different from your own must refer to an autobiography or a biography that you have studied.

Commentary: It could be the story of someone famous or someone ordinary, even disturbed, such as the character Stuart in the biography *Stuart: A Life Backwards* by Alexander Masters, an unusually structured book and one which is very readable.

Section C – Poetry

12. From time to time, there is a question inviting candidates to talk about form – and this is it.

Commentary: You shouldn't be afraid of questions about poetic and linguistic techniques. There is a sense in which the question implies something blatantly obvious: what else is there for a poem's success to depend on? What makes poetry poetic and memorable are the techniques – such as rhyme, rhythm, versification, imagery, linguistic devices. The forcing of sentence structure into a regular rhythm and regular rhyme by the use of caesura and enjambement, for example, is what makes 'My Last Duchess' so successful. Not only that, but the tendency to read the poem in sentences causes the rhyme to go unnoticed, thus in a sense symbolising the Duke's deeply embedded nastiness.

Furthermore, 'My Last Duchess' depends on the rhyme and also the rhythm. You should know the meaning of iambic pentameter: the weak/strong weak/strong beat employed by so many poets, including Shakespeare. Iambic is the rhythm of everyday speech. For example, take the following two sentences:

> Let's **go** and **have** a **cup** of **coff**ee.
> We'll **take** our **dog** to **see** the **vet** to**day**.

Say these sentences out loud, emphasising the emboldened words. That's a rhythm that you find natural to you – and note how it stresses the important words.

Now look at the opening lines of the poem that you are studying. Here is the opening line of 'My Last Duchess':

> That's **my** last **duch**ess **paint**ed **on** the **wall**,

It's a perfect example of iambic pentameter (Pentameter means there are five such weak/strong beats in a line.). But look at the next two lines. The stress has been made where it should come naturally:

> Look**ing** as **if** she **were** a**live**; **I** call
> That **piece** a **won**der, **now**: **Fra** Pan**dolf's** hands
> Worked **busily** a **day**, and **there** she **stands**.

If you say the lines as though they were all iambic pentameter, you would fracture the sense. After the break – what's called the caesura – the iamb is often reversed, as it is in both cases here. And that means that the caesura and the inversion cause the speaker to pause, reflecting the rhythm of everyday speech, and forcing the enjambement. You don't notice the rhyming of 'wall' and 'call'.

It's the same in the next two lines – after 'now:' the colon forces a pause, followed by inversion so that we have to say the lines – 'Fra Pandolf's hands worked busily a day', ignoring the line break, which means you follow the sentence structure and not the line structure. It sounds more like everyday speech and hides the rhyming of 'hands' and 'stands'.

Because there are five such weak/strong beats in each line we call the rhythm iambic pentameter. Were there three such beats it would be iambic trimeter, and four such beats it would be iambic tetrameter.

Just remember that after a caesura there is often inversion of the iambic foot.

13. Be careful of the references to 'you' in Critical Essay questions: it isn't really an invitation for you to write about yourself – it is a wording examiners use to try to make sure you can relate to the ideas in the question. The best advice is not to refer to yourself but refer instead to 'the reader' or even 'we'.

This is the particular/universal question cropping up in poetry. It is a common question, but then what it states is true of all literature – a text is about the particular but it also has universal significance.

Commentary: You are limited a bit by the 'everyday' experience – you couldn't really, for example, claim that war is an everyday experience, though it was for the war poets. It would be safer, however, to deal with a poem that clearly is about the everyday – a poem such as 'In the Snack Bar' by Edwin Morgan would be a good one to choose.

Let's take 'Waiting Room' by Moira Andrew – in a sense an everyday experience because it concerns the persona's visit to a nursing home to see a relative. The question is about the poet's skill – in other words, you have to examine how the poet uses poetic and linguistic techniques to make this everyday experience appeal to a wider audience.

Andrew's skill lies in her ability to make the audience feel sympathy for the old lady – through images of her room being 'tight with memories/claustrophobic with possessions'. She has taken with her as much as she can and the room is so full that it is difficult to move. That, in itself, makes you feel sympathy for her – that an elderly person has to reduce his or her life to a room full of memories. But, furthermore, the imagery she uses to convey the appearance of the old lady – 'bone-china thin', where 'bone-china' not only conveys the fragility of the old lady but, since we associate bone china with her generation, the image also conveys her age.

But the real universal significance of the poem comes in the last verse, where Andrew uses the pathetic fallacy to convey the pathos of old age. The repetition of 'waiting' conveys the emptiness of the old woman's life in the nursing home – the parenthetical '(Saturday, boiled eggs for tea)' draws attention to the fact that all she has to look forward to on a Saturday evening is boiled eggs. But what also is very effective is the way in which she manages to convey the different shades of meaning of 'waiting' as she repeats the word throughout the verse. The 'waiting to obey the gong' is very finite and fixed, whereas 'waiting for the rain to stop' less so in that you can't be sure when it will end. But the 'waiting for winter' creates such sympathy since the repetition in the line of the word 'waiting' and the alliteration which draws our attention to it combine to make us realise that 'winter' is ambiguous. It also suggests dying.

There are many poems that seem to begin with an everyday experience, but their true success lies in the poet's ability to infuse them with universal significance.

14. Again, think not so much about how 'you' find the poem meaningful, but how the reader might.

Many poems, too, are the result of a poet's experience of loss.

Commentary: But remember that part of the skill in writing Critical Essays is the ability to widen the topic. The idea of loss can be taken in several ways: of course, we immediately think of the loss of a person, but it could be the loss of an animal, a house or even a season. 'Ode to Autumn' by Keats, you could argue, is really about the loss of autumn (for him and for all of us). But there is a poem by Elizabeth Bishop called 'One Art', and it is devoted to the idea of loss. Her first verse makes it clear that the poem is about just that.

She claims that:

> The art of losing isn't hard to master;
> so many things seem filled with the intent
> to be lost that their loss is no disaster.

She goes on and talks about losing trivial things, such as keys, an 'hour badly spent'; she talks of losing her mother's watch, and losing a continent (by leaving, presumably).

The last verse is particularly poignant:

> —Even losing you (the joking voice, a gesture
> I love) I shan't have lied. It's evident
> the art of losing's not too hard to master
> though it may look like (*Write it!*) like disaster.

It's as though the persona has to force herself to accept the disaster of losing someone she loved.

15. The poems that can communicate menace are many and varied: from ballads to, certainly, poetry of the late 20th century.

Commentary: Maybe it would be worth your while studying some ballads. 'Edward Edward', the Scots version, is a particularly menacing poem, but so are some of the poems of Edwin Muir – 'The Combat' and 'The Castle'. Also the poems of Ted Hughes, particularly 'The Jaguar', 'Thrushes' and 'Pike', convey menace at various levels.

Section D – Film and TV Drama

16. Of late, there has been a plethora of film and TV dramas about the future – which may say something about the need to escape from the discomfort felt by society in the early 21st century!

Commentary: You have to show *how* the film/programme makers make it clear that it is in the future, which means that you need to be aware of the devices used to imply the future – and remember the future may not be a pleasant or a prosperous one. Next you have to indicate the ways in which the film or programme engaged your interest and made the future plausible.

The problem is that the future (as envisaged by the imagination) has to be based on the present. Objects, people, even aliens have to be based on what we know and understand. It is impossible to create a future that has in it beings or objects or structures that are not already present – we can't invent something totally original and alien. Therefore the skill of the directors has to be focused on probability – making the programme believable. That is at the heart of this question.

17. Programmes and films that try to portray historical events are also popular – think of the many films and programmes that there have been about Queen Elizabeth I or Queen Victoria or either of the two World Wars.

Commentary: The question is asking you to examine how the programme makers make everything seem real and not just like a museum piece that moves. Also, as with films and programmes about the future, how do they manage to make films and programmes about the past seem relevant?

> **HINT** Relevance is not, of course, ever clear cut – what was relevant at the turn of this millennium may not be as relevant today as something that took place at the turn of the 18th century. Maybe you should begin by making a comment on what you mean by relevance.

18. The failure can be about anything – but most likely it will be failure to achieve something that a main character sees as important.

> **HINT** One man's failure can easily been seen by another as success or vice versa – it may be wise for you to define how you are going to interpret failure.

Commentary: Many film and TV dramas, especially American ones, don't relish failure. American material tends to end happily, everything coated in cloying sentiment. But British film and TV drama does not shy away from disappointment and breakdown.

The question invites you to consider setting as well as characterisation, which means that failure can be failure to achieve something physical.

19. This is a fairly standard Critical Essay question that can crop up in the drama and fiction sections as well as here.

Commentary: You have to deal with the ways in which the director has created build-up to this crucial scene and, then, you have to deal with the ways in which the scene is a turning point for both character and plot. Most probably the two are connected in that the change brought about in the plot is bound to affect the fortune of the protagonist.